Setting a Sustainable Trajectory

Setting a Sustainable Trajectory
A Pedagogical Theory for Christian Worldview Formation

Rob Lindemann

WIPF & STOCK · Eugene, Oregon

SETTING A SUSTAINABLE TRAJECTORY
A Pedagogical Theory for Christian Worldview Formation

Copyright © 2018 Rob Lindemann. All rights reserved. Except for brief quotations in critical publications or reviews, no part of this book may be reproduced in any manner without prior written permission from the publisher. Write: Permissions, Wipf and Stock Publishers, 199 W. 8th Ave., Suite 3, Eugene, OR 97401.

Wipf & Stock
An Imprint of Wipf and Stock Publishers
199 W. 8th Ave., Suite 3
Eugene, OR 97401

www.wipfandstock.com

PAPERBACK ISBN: 978-1-5326-3574-8
HARDCOVER ISBN: 978-1-5326-3576-2
EBOOK ISBN: 978-1-5326-3575-5

Manufactured in the U.S.A.

This book is dedicated to the memory of my father, John Richard Lindemann, who passed away during its completion.

Contents

List of Illustrations and Tables | ix
Acknowledgments | xi
Introduction | xiii

Chapter 1: Introduction to the Research | 1
    Statement of the Problem   4
    Research Questions   5
    Key Terms   5
    Limitations and Delimitations   6
    Significance of this Research   8
    Summary   9

Chapter 2: Review of the Literature | 10
    The Role of Worldview in Education   10
    How Worldviews Develop and Change   17
    Subject Areas Most Related to Worldview Formation   22
    The Belief Characteristics of Teachers and Students   23
    Instructional and Assessment Strategies in the Field   27
    Gaps in the Literature   36
    Summary and Conclusion   37

Chapter 3: Research Methodology | 39
    Introduction   39
    Setting and Context   42
    Participants and Sampling Strategy   44

CONTENTS

Research Design, Data Collection,
    and Analytical Procedures 45
Role of the Researcher and Bracketing 50
Research Ethics 51
Potential Contribution of the Research 52

Chapter 4: Research Findings | 53
Introduction 53
Initial and Focused Coding 59
Analysis of the Data 61
Emergent Themes 75
Summary 80

Chapter 5: Discussions and Conclusion | 82
Question One: Instructional Design and
    Pedagogical Methods 83
Question Two: The Teacher's Worldview and
    Relationship with Students 88
Question Three: Assessing Worldview Awareness
    and Development 89
Proposed Model for Worldview Pedagogy
    in Bible Colleges 90
Conclusion 95
Recommendations for Further Study 96

Appendix A: Interview Guide Questions | 99

*Appendix B: Email Request for Letter of Cooperation
    —President or Dean* | 100

Appendix C: Letter of Consent—Participant | 102

Bibliography | 105

Illustrations and Tables

Table 1. Summary of Interview Participants | 54

Figure 1. A Model for Christian Worldview Pedagogy | 94

Acknowledgments

I WOULD LIKE TO thank the following people for their support during my doctoral education program:

To my faculty advisor, Dr. Gary Tiffin, for his consistent availability and thoughtful counsel during the challenging times of this doctoral journey. May you enjoy your retirement!

To my committee chair Dr. Patrick Allen for his tremendous personal support, winsome humor, and scholarly guidance as chair of my dissertation committee. I look forward to reading all your future books.

To Dr. Ken Badley and Dr. Terry Huffman for their superb examples of scholarship and expertise in helping shape this research. Your professionalism will inspire me for years to come.

To the 2014 EdD program cohort members whose company I enjoyed during two summers on campus in Newberg, OR. They provided a great deal encouragement and a much needed sense of inclusion. It was an honor to share this journey together.

Most of all, I want to thank my loving wife Debra and my children, Nathan and Emily, for their patient support over the full duration of my post-secondary education since it began in 1997. To my children especially, since your birth you have always seen me involved in some type of educational program. I hope the completion of my doctoral degree and this book inspires belief that you could do the same one day. Remember, with God all things are possible (cf. Matthew 19:26).

Introduction

To date, only emerging qualitative data exist on pedagogy employed specifically for worldview formation, especially in Christian contexts. Using a grounded theory approach, I carried out this qualitative research using personal interviews for the purpose of discovering a theory for the processes expert teachers use in employing effective worldview pedagogy. Data were gathered through personal interviews with six participants who were nominated by their presidents or deans as suitable candidates according to the criteria of an expert teacher in this aspect of Bible college teaching.

The process of qualitative coding led to a pedagogical theory for Christian worldview formation characterized by four themes: a) setting clarity on what aspect of worldview formation the teacher aims to develop; b) designing relevant holistic objectives that bring coherence between the world the student experiences and the Christian values that apply to it; c) using teaching methods that move along a continuum of deconstruction and reconstruction strategies along with active learning exercises that help set a trajectory for students' ongoing worldview development; and d) compiling assessment data from tools that focus on specific areas of worldview development and measure small gains in keeping with an appropriate pace of formation.

1

Introduction to the Research

EDUCATING FOR CHRISTIAN WORLDVIEW formation is often concerned with teaching the basic tenets of Christianity that differentiate it from other worldviews. Such training tends to be heavily propositional and cognitive, with less attention given to the experiential and practical (Mittwede, 2013). Other approaches emphasize the quantity of theological learning as the determining factor in shaping worldview. It is as though some educators presume a linear model whereby if a critical mass of conceptual change occurs in the student, then the sheer force of theological weight will shift his or her worldview to a biblical or Christian orientation.

Many educational philosophers dismiss the notion of value-free education, acknowledging that all subjects are taught from a particular worldview. For example, Nash (2003) describes value-free education as a myth that supposedly ensures students freedom from coerced exposure to someone else's values. In fact, Belcher and Parr (2011) claim that everything an institution does teaches values and worldview in both explicit and implicit ways. Together, these define for students what can be known in the world and how it can be known, what ought to be done in a given situation, and what goals are worth pursuing (Koltko-Rivera, 2004).

The factual transmission of such content does play an essential role in forming a person's worldview. However, what pedagogical factors and strategies do teachers consider when designing and assessing effective worldview learning? For example, the Worldview Explorations curriculum from the Institute of Noetic Sciences offers a developmental model based on pedagogical research in consciousness and transformation. The program, which is for middle school, high school, and college students, uses self-reflective practices and project-based group activities to blend intellectual development with emotional and social intelligence. In addition, Jordan, Bawden, and Bergmann (2008) offer one of the most rigorous studies on worldview pedagogy, but it is set in the agroecosystem context and the challenges of sustainability due to the expanding range of goods and services agriculture offers to society. They address the challenges agricultural professionals will face as new innovations in ecological services bring them into critical civic debates that require a capacity to facilitate both "challenges to, and where appropriate, changes in prevailing worldviews—their own as well as those of others" (2008, p. 92). To prepare for such encounters, the authors emphasize a pedagogy that equips students' individual capacities to think and act systemically as well as their collective capacities (i.e., social learning) for navigating moral and practical issues brought by the increasing complexities and controversies in this industry.

What is motivating the research attention paid to the pedagogy employed in these types of programs? Schlitz and her colleagues capture it well, saying:

> Today globalization, technology, and urbanization increasingly draw together divergent cultures and connect previously isolated regions in ways that have never occurred before. The rate at which information is accumulated and accessed has grown exponentially, challenging us to see the world with new eyes and to adapt our educational systems to meet demands that were inconceivable in the previous era. A growing number of educators and researchers are suggesting that it is no longer possible to separate training of the intellect from the cultivation of emotional and social intelligence. We need to focus not simply on acquiring information, but on understanding ourselves as learners. (2011, para. 5)

Many industries recognize that the way they present themselves and interact with others is equally important as the product or service they provide society. This realization is presented as a type of literacy and often appears in educational discussions about developing "21st-century skills," which refers to a broad set of knowledge, learning habits, and character traits thought to be vital for success in emerging society. Increasingly, these industries and their educators are turning to pedagogical strategies for raising students' worldview consciousness and shaping their individual and social capacities for providing moral leadership that builds peaceful, cooperative communities amidst the variety of ethical perspectives and conflict that comes with increasing diversity.

To date, only emergent qualitative data exist on pedagogy employed specifically for worldview formation, especially in Christian contexts. Some of these studies explore pedagogical implications for the shaping and expression of Christian worldview in professional studies programs such as counseling (Grauf-Grounds, Edwards, Macdonald, Mui-Teng Quek, & Schermer Sellers, 2009; Wolf, 2011) and management studies (Daniels, Franz, & Wong, 2000). Some notable doctoral dissertations have recently appeared focusing on pedagogy in the K-12 Christian school setting (Fyock, 2008; Wood, 2008) as well as the Christian college situation (Brickhill, 2010; Wilkie, 2015), while others give attention to testing the reliability of tools for assessing Christian worldview in university students (Morales, 2013). Finally, recent studies have appeared that develop cognitive theoretical frameworks combined with active learning methods for provoking deeper worldview development (Collier & Dowson, 2008; Mittwede, 2013; Ter Avest, Bertram-Troost, & Miedema, 2012).

Two main contributions to the literature influence this project. First, I use the monograph by Kanitz (2005) as a point of departure because she first called for improvements to Christian worldview pedagogy. Like many teachers, she presents the context of Christian higher education as a powerful opportunity to develop a greater vibrancy and holistic worldview in students. Yet many educators are uncertain about teaching and assessment methods they can use for this elusive objective. Kanitz also highlights important pedagogical factors that make this a challenge, such as the multiplicity of Christian worldviews to consider, the influence of denominational and institutional traditions, the ambiguity of assessment, the tendency toward pluralism influenced by postmodern forms of thinking, and the hermeneutical approaches students take to reading and interpreting the Bible.

Second, Ward (2012) provides a helpful perspective on curriculum planning that sees no bifurcation between what should be taught and why. To emphasize his point, he deliberately uses awkward grammar by asking "What should be taught why?" (i.e., no "and" between "taught" and "why"). In doing so, he underscores that teachers should always plan the subject being taught in the context of why it should be taught. Similarly, this study underscores that teachers must also plan the subject being taught in the context of how it should be taught (i.e., the pedagogy). This study assumes that teachers can shape and strengthen a Christian worldview within several disciplines. Therefore, in a style like Ward, this research seeks to answer the question, "What should be taught how?"

Statement of the Problem

Because no theory exists to explain how an expert teacher shapes the Christian worldview of college students, I carried out this qualitative research using personal interviews with six faculty members from Bible colleges accredited with the Association for Biblical Higher Education. The purpose was to discover the notable pedagogical factors, instructional strategies, and assessment approaches they use in their teaching ministry. In keeping with the objective of grounded theory, I examined these aspects so a theory of effective worldview pedagogy could emerge from the data. This study adds to the literature on Christian worldview by offering a theoretical framework for instructional design that is intended to shape the Christian worldview of college students.

The literature thus far on this subject tends to emphasize phenomenological perspectives (Belcher & Parr, 2011; Mittwede, 2013; Setran, Wilhoit, Ratcliff, Haase, & Rozema, 2010) while other disciplines have explored it through a grounded theory approach (Daniels et al., 2000; Jordan et al., 2008). The concerns and observations raised by Kanitz (2005) have been cited in four studies in the past two years (D. M. Carpenter, 2015; Chan & Wong, 2014; Morales, 2013; Wilkie, 2015). This study adds to the literature by situating its context in undergraduate Bible college education.

Research Questions

For this qualitative study, I explored these research questions that align with the selected problem and intent of the study:

1. What instructional designs and pedagogical methods are especially effective for raising worldview awareness and shaping Christian worldview development?
2. How does the worldview of the teacher and his or her relationships with students influence pedagogical effectiveness?
3. How are teachers assessing college students for worldview awareness and development?

Key Terms

Assessment: Involves the gathering and analysis of empirical data on student learning for refining academic programs and improving student learning (Allen, 2003).

Association for Biblical Higher Education (ABHE): A North American accrediting agency comprised of approximately 200 postsecondary institutions throughout North America that specialize in biblical and theological studies as well as professional ministry training.

Christian worldview: A worldview shaped by theological and biblical precepts understood within a particular Christian tradition and cultural setting.

Instructional design: The development of learning experiences and environments that incorporate known and verified learning strategies into instructional experiences which make holistic learning more efficient, effective, and appealing (Merrill, Drake, Lacy, & Pratt, 1996).

Pedagogy: Depending on its use or context, pedagogy refers to the craft, science, practice, or profession of teaching, especially concerning principles and methods of teaching. Expressions include formal classroom/curricular instruction, co-curricular activities, accompanying, and caring for students.

Strategies and factors: A thoughtful and responsive plan or method of instruction that incorporates known circumstances, facts, or influences contributing to a condition or outcome.

Worldview: For the purposes of this study, I will use this concise yet broad definition, which allows the interview participants to shape its meaning more as they see it: A worldview is comprised of the beliefs, values, assumptions, and volitions that provide the rationale for how people understand and order their lives.

Worldview pedagogy: Teaching and learning that aims to develop not only traditional cognitive faculties but also crucial aspects such as social, moral, and spiritual development that take place in other non-academic areas of the college experience.

Limitations and Delimitations

An inherent limitation with qualitative research is that the sample cannot be generalized to a larger population. I intentionally chose a small sample to learn about the experiences and views of expert faculty in accredited Bible colleges who, according to their presidents and deans (i.e., gatekeepers), have been especially effective in shaping the Christian worldview of their students. The notion of what constitutes an expert in this type of instruction is also a limitation, despite noteworthy research done on this level of ability in other educational contexts (e.g., Hattie & Jaeger, 2003). To assist with this issue, I offered gatekeepers some criteria observed in the literature from which they could consider a nominee. Another limitation is that gatekeepers nominated faculty based on their observations and opinions on what constitutes effectiveness in this type of instruction. Nevertheless, the purpose of this research was to determine what factors these teachers consider, what instructional design direction they take, and what methods of assessment they employ.

Research using a grounded theory approach is valuable for rich exploration of a topic, especially where a clear theory is not yet established. As a result, this approach does rely on interpretative skills from the researcher to define and redefine the meanings of what they observe and hear (Stake, 2010). Therefore, the rigor of this study was dependent on my ability as the researcher to bracket my own professional biases and rely upon my adherence and commitment to rich, thick description as part of validation.

Delimitations include the sample coming only from Bible colleges in Canada and the United States that are accredited with the Association of Biblical Higher Education (ABHE). Therefore, neither the perspectives of non-North American educators nor teachers outside of accredited higher education were included in this study. Theory testing with a larger sample of schools and within broader socioeconomic and cultural settings will provide better understanding of pedagogical factors and strategies that could strengthen theoretical understanding for professional practice.

For convenience, the sample was also delimited to certain affiliated church traditions. Given that ABHE affirms tenets of faith that are broadly Protestant, member colleges come from this Western church tradition. Nevertheless, I took measures to ensure diverse theological representation of the Protestant tradition in the sample.

A final delimitation was that the participants must have been contemporary, active professors. As a result, recently retired or former teachers were not included even though they certainly could have offered some insights. The sample interviewed was delimited to those nominated and did not include the perspectives of students. While the views of students would be helpful to include it is beyond the scope of this research to include this sample. Chapter five addresses suggestions for further research, which includes students as a unit of analysis.

Significance of this Research

This study of pedagogical expertise in Christian worldview formation is significant for many of the same reasons observed by Schlitz and her colleagues (2011). Educating for this worldview and the interests of biblical higher education face similar challenges inherent with the gathering of diverse cultures into closer contact and increased connection with previously isolated people groups. Thus, Christian education shares similar theoretical constructs with secular education researchers. For example, training the intellect together with the cultivation of emotional and social intelligence is in keeping with Hiebert's (2005) description of the Bible college movement's focus on character development and ministry competence.

The key difference lies in the worldview under development, which guides students to live according to its assumptions and values. In addition, the way a teacher sees their role matters greatly and reflects a certain worldview. For example, Knight (2006) believes that Christian education should be considered a redemptive act because it involves restoring the image of God in students. If viewed that way, then the role of a teacher becomes an agent of reconciliation representing God's interests and acting as catalyst in that transformation. Effective teaching in this context then becomes a spiritual and social responsibility essential to the character formation of students (Fong, 2009).

INTRODUCTION TO THE RESEARCH

Summary

This chapter establishes the background and purpose for this qualitative study based on personal interviews with expert teachers. I transcribed and reviewed the interviews for deep familiarization, coded and delineated them for themes, and then pulled the findings together into a concluding theory. The next chapter's literature review explores the concept of worldview in both historical overview and pedagogical application within the educational context. The focus is primarily on phenomenological studies and grounded theory approaches. These studies provide support for continuing professional competence in teachers and developing theory and policies that shape both curriculum design and teaching practices.

2

Review of the Literature

WORLDVIEWS ARE COMPRISED OF beliefs, values, assumptions, and volitions that provide the rationale for how people understand and order their lives. The influence of a person's worldview can be conscious or unconscious and is associated with educational issues such as identity formation, approaches to ethics and problem-solving, understanding systemic relationships, and citizenship (Jordan et al., 2008; Matthews, 2009a). The concept has significant importance in Christian education to the point that several institutions claim the formation and guiding assumptions of a Christian worldview are central to their mission (Grauf-Grounds et al., 2009; Kanitz, 2005).

This review of the literature presents prominent factors and strategies discussed in the research on pedagogy and Christian worldview. Several empirical studies and monographs are explored with four main themes emerging: a) the role of worldview in education, b) subject areas most related to worldview formation; c) the belief characteristics of teachers and students, and d) instructional and assessment strategies in the field.

The Role of Worldview in Education

Educators often consider worldview something implicit and integral in the processes and outcomes of learning in a variety of subjects (Daniels et al., 2000; Matthews, 2009b). Williams offers a concise conceptual definition of a worldview as "a set of concepts that assembles everything else we believe into a coherent whole" (2002, p. 18), thus positioning the idea within the pursuit of coherence (i.e., internal agreement). A person's worldview informs his or her notion of reality as well as their approaches to theory, methods, analyses, and interpretation of data (Tudge, 2000). As Baumann points out, worldviews "provide for the majority of individuals in society, not only a descriptive and normative vision of life, but also framework for developing ways of operating in the world" (2011, p. 9). Even spiritual formation studies flow from this broader and more foundational framework (Setran et al., 2010; Shimabukuro, 2008). As Bufford puts it, "Worldviews are like sand at a picnic; they get into everything" (2007, p. 293).

Many scholars use the term *worldview* to translate from German the words *Weltanschauung* and *Weltbild,* although the latter translates better as "world picture" in English. The German historian and philosopher Wilhelm Dilthey (d. 1911) was the first to use these terms when he constructed a typology for conceiving views of humankind's relationship to nature. Through the writings of several key thinkers, this period also gave rise to several related ideas such as *Weltauffassung, Weltansicht,* and *Lebensanschauung* (Badii & Fabbri, 2011). Dilthey's goal was to expand Kant's primarily cognitive-focused *Critique of Pure Reason,* first published in 1781, to do justice to the full scope of human lived experience. Dilthey felt this new critique must proceed based on the psychological laws and impulses from which art, religion, and science all derive (Makkreel, Summer 2012 Edition). In fact, he sought to interpret various phenomena of religious experience a few times in his writings. Dolan reports that Dilthey claimed the purpose of a worldview was "to illustrate the relationship of the human mind to the riddles of the world and life" (2010, p. 16).

In the preface to the *Introduction to the Human Sciences* (1989), Dilthey refers to his project as a "Critique of Historical Reason," positing a worldview typology as "typical" to life (as opposed to Max Weber's notion of "ideal types") in three categories representing not just a rational pattern, but a total life-attitude as organizing centers:

- Naturalism—wherein people see themselves as determined by nature.
- Idealism of Freedom—wherein people are conscious of their separation from nature by their own free will.
- Objective idealism—wherein people are conscious of their harmony with nature.

In recent years, the secular humanist tradition of philosophy and education has used closely related terms such as consciousness (Schlitz, Vieten, & Amorok, 2007), lifestance, or eupraxsophy (Kurtz, 1994) in parallel discussions on social wellbeing, ethics, and exuberant living.

Several Christian theologians and philosophers in the first half of the 20th century adapted Dilthey's ideas in forming the worldview concept to fit within their theistic framework (Wood, 2008). Some of the most notable include James Orr, Abraham Kuyper, and Herman Depowered (Dolan, 2010; Naugle, 2002; Sire, 2009). Since that time, discussions and education related to the Christian worldview have employed two common metaphors: a) seeing—a way of viewing the world, and b) walking—a manner of living in the world (Kanitz, 2005). A great deal of attention to Christian worldview has occurred over the past three decades, focusing on two primary emphases: a) conceptual discussion and refinement (Bertrand, 2007; Naugle, 2002; Sire, 2004; Walsh & Middleton, 1984), and b) apologetics-oriented analysis and response training for understanding competing worldviews (Burnett, 1990; Geisler & Watkins, 1989; Nash, 1992; Sire, 2009; Wilkens & Sanford, 2009).

Reception to the term "worldview" across Christian education traditions ranges from strong adherence to ambivalence, which has produced a lack of conceptual consistency. Kanitz (2005) acknowledges that there are, in fact, multiple Christian worldviews due to differences in our interpretive communities. Evangelicals, for example, tend to position the concept within intellectual discussions on the integration of faith and learning (Badley, 1994; Harris, 2004). Conversely, non-Reformed traditions such as Catholic,

Wesleyan, Lutheran, Pentecostal, or Anabaptists are not as comfortable with an integrationist approach, preferring the "walking" metaphor with its emphasis on faith in action.

de Oliveira (2006) adds a key point by positing limitations to the two major terms used most often by Christian writers: Christian Worldview and Biblical Worldview. He believes the former tends to use an idealistic, philosophical, and intellectual approach while the latter emphasizes a scriptural and expositional approach. The author proposes that the term "Biblically Shaped Worldview" is more accurate and preferable because it "frees the church in various cultural settings to be united in Christ, but still maintain its cultural identity and peculiarities" (de Oliveira, 2006, p. 176).

Naugle (2002) points out in his historical overview that the Reformed tradition have struggled with the suitability of the worldview concept for use in Christian discussions because of its nuances of relativism. Therefore, he proposes a four-part process to naturalize the worldview idea for Christian usage that works for Reformers. However, broader buy-in to the conceptualization of worldview reaches limitations when scholars take a hyper-philosophical approach that requires professional educators to think more like philosophers instead of instructional designers (Jacobsen & Jacobsen, 2004). Nevertheless, educating for worldview formation does need to wrestle with important philosophical ideas and goals that are already influencing students by the time they arrive in the college setting. This period in their lives is vital because many are emerging into or even re-shaping their adult identities. In fact, C. Smith (2009) refers to typical college-aged students as "souls in transition." Once in the classroom, teachers enter intellectual and practical ground already populated with various worldviews firmly entrenched and competition for developing a faith stance is tight (Kanitz, 2005; Setran & Kiesling, 2013).

Jacobsen and Jacobsen (2004) argue that the integrationist model in Reformed theology has made scholars too combative with the rest of the academic world. They caution that the worldview concept is losing its former power due to a shift in academia away from all-inclusive theorizing about the nature of the world to smaller-scale aspects examined eclectically. They say this shift is moving away from precise, bilateral, Cold War thinking (i.e., an inability to give up balance-of-power politics) to something more decentered, multilateral, and postmodern in orientation. The authors write:

> Contemporary ways of thought and life are less concerned with the norms of logic favored by the worldview approach and much more concerned with the quirky and often unpredictable ways things actually fit together in their local and global environments. (2004, pp. 27-28)

The authors acknowledge that the traditional abstract, overarching approach to worldview from the integrationist perspective still has value, but suggest that scholars must develop more specific, relatable ways to integrate faith and learning.

A key educational benefit to worldview study is that it makes a person alert to the presuppositions they hold as well as those of others. A lack of such awareness can cause significant personal and social bewilderment. Edlin (2009) compares this to the official versus operational curricula in a typical school. He says the former appears on school websites, accreditation reports, and catalogues stating what the school will do for students. On the other hand, the operational curriculum is what happens in the classroom and general school ethos. The two curricula can be quite dissimilar, which Edlin says can also happen with a person's Christian worldview. For example, a Christian can claim a biblically faithful worldview yet, at the same time, be vulnerable to deceptive cultural influences that make their operational lives quite inconsistent with biblical truth (see e.g., Wilkens & Sanford, 2009). Another caution for teachers is equating doctrinal assent with spiritual advancement or worldview change (Mittwede, 2013). Transformation differs from intellectual agreement, although the latter is easier to assess.

Similarly, Belcher (2009) explores the question whether the core of education is really the education of the heart. It is a foundational question based on Naugle's (2004) premise of human life proceeding *kardioptically*, which means out of a vision of an embodied heart living in the world. Belcher's intent is to use narrative inquiry to explore what impact a Christian educational institute has on adherents over time. She hopes to describe ways in which one specific Christian institution does or does not live up to its mission statement by examining the worldview/values/praxis of its alumni. Her research seeks to understand spiritual and kardioptic worldview literacy, though as of this date she has not yet published her findings.

Emphasizing students' affective formation before their cognitive formation resembles J. K. A. Smith's (2009) work where he argues that contemporary Christian education focuses too much on worldview analysis and integration. Instead, he insists that we "feel our way around our world more than we think our way through it. Our worldview is more a matter of the imagination than the intellect, and the imagination runs off the fuel of images that are channeled by the senses" (2009, p. 57). He calls those images *pre-cognitive drivers* that lead us to worship before we ever articulate a worldview. Smith claims that pedagogical approaches that fail to incorporate embodiment and practices of worship tend to default to propositional and cognitive concepts of worldview (cf. Mittwede, 2013). Nevertheless, while Smith acknowledges the importance of the latter aspects, his point is that teachers should "*situate* the cognitive, propositional aspects of Christian faith [as that which emerges] in and from practices" (2009, p. 191). Thus, he insists, Christian colleges should be suffused with ecclesiastical liturgies alongside and within academic study to influence students' pre-conscious desires as they shape the more intellectual aspects of worldview formation.

Certain theological themes play a role in designing strategies and outcomes in Christian education. Daniels and her colleagues (2000) are guided by two main themes: a) understanding of the nature and condition of humankind as both made in God's image yet corrupted by sin, and b) recognizing the nature of community as based in reconciliation with God through Jesus Christ. As a result, they use teaching strategies that encourage students to recognize the behaviors they choose both reflect and contribute to the development of their character. Students are also encouraged to appreciate they exist in an interdependent web of relationships. Smithwick (2004) however focuses on the nature of truth as interpreted through that the Bible. Therefore, learning outcomes are centered on how Scripture guides ethical, moral, and legal reasoning as well as reinforcing the truth God has revealed as absolute for all times.

Resolving basic educational problems often involve interdisciplinary cooperation and multiple perspectives (Matthews, 2009; Tudge, 2000). These perspectives are open to challenge and, at times, require change. Therefore, raising worldview consciousness is critical for these interactions. For example, Jordan, Bawden and Bergmann (2008) designed a university course to equip students for critical engagement with others around collective learning. Their approach teaches students how to learn cooperatively and appreciate various levels of cognition as they make inter-connections in systems of learning. This approach allows students to demonstrate greater appreciation for the characteristics of worldviews and differing perspectives along with the tensions involved when exploring complex issues.

Koltko-Rivera (2004) brings up a key point central to this topic that he calls *worldview malleability*, which is a characteristic that affects all deliberate efforts to influence or change a person's worldview. The idea is important in education as well as many other disciplines including counseling and clinical psychology, health, peace, and educational psychology. His primary concern is with comparing how worldviews are similar, or different, to other beliefs and attitudes in resisting attempts to change them. While a copious amount of literature exists regarding attitude change, that knowledge has yet to be extended specifically to the matter of worldview malleability. Similarly, de Oliviera (2006) acknowledges that a person's worldview does not completely change once becoming a Christian. Rather, it transforms while at the same time retaining certain cultural and even theological diversities.

Although classroom pedagogy involves a strong cognitive component, crucial aspects of worldview formation, such as social, moral, and spiritual development, can take place in other areas of the college experience (Sherr, Huff, & Curran, 2007). Krakowski (2008) even argues that a worldview emerges from both the activities individuals engage in and the beliefs they maintain. Schlitz, Vieten, and Miller (2010) explore a similar focus concentrating on the role of worldview transformation as it relates to developing explicit social consciousness. They claim that as worldviews transform, they adapt to include increasing levels of awareness of how people are interrelated to the world around them, which then influences prosocial perceptions and actions—an objective that shares much in common with Christian higher education. Given their research aims at developing social consciousness, it is not surprising this methodology resembles a progressive educational philosophy using cognitive constructivist learning theories. Overall, several aspects of the educational experience are influential to worldview formation including co-curricular programming, which can focus on distinct educational goals.

Overall, faculty seeking to integrate faith and learning must begin by clarifying their assumptions behind the Christian worldview because, as Kanitz (2005) points out, there are no universally agreed upon criteria. Therefore, she cautions teachers about presenting Christian worldview as a unified concept. As a result, encouraging students to think Christianly about a subject requires educational approaches that raise consciousness of an array of influences and processes by which a person determines a biblical principle (Kanitz, 2005).

How Worldviews Develop and Change

The literature often focuses on the descriptive and normative functions of a worldview. However, this research builds upon other works that examine the educational processes of worldview development. For example, Baumann (2011) states that a worldview develops as part of the essence of being human; therefore, it is also a socio-psychological process. He explains that the worldview a person initially adopts is largely determinative, i.e., based on the foremost perspective of the culture into which he or she is born. He explains further:

> As we interact with people who are more competent because of experience and greater socialization in the dominant worldview, we begin to assimilate the cultural tools (i.e., the values, attitudes, language, customs, etc.) that allow us to interact with the world and people in meaningful and predictable ways. (Baumann, 2011, p. 19)

A worldview changes in conjunction with other key areas, such as cognitive, moral, social, and intellectual development, as well as a person's socialization into a culture. Hiebert (2008) agrees with these areas but also includes the affective (feelings) and evaluative (norms and decision-making) aspects of transformation. He also acknowledges that, in general, worldviews change in either one of two ways: through growth processes or some type of radical shift.

Kennedy and Humphreys (1994) address this in the context of therapy of psychological healing, pointing out that worldviews typically change as people become more active interpreters of their environments. Conversely, worldview change also occurs with reactions to traumatic events because these experiences have power to alter a person's unconscious assumptions. The authors point out that successful recovery from such events requires a conscious examination of these assumptions under the care of a professional and/or in mutual help groups. In addition, they insist that worldview change involves more than just beliefs. Important behavioral changes such as abstaining from substance abuse, practicing more prosocial relational skills, or acting with greater integrity and honesty tend to accompany modified beliefs with major worldview changes.

Baumann (2011) discusses worldview development by first referring to Wolterstorff's (1999) ideas about data beliefs and control beliefs as each relates to knowledge acquisition. The latter are presuppositions or assumptions taken to be true and thus do not need to be defended or supported. Wolterstorff claims that a worldview becomes established in a person when control beliefs and their corresponding values are reinforced by a particular communal group. As a result, Baumann explores how control beliefs come to be by first referencing developmental psychologists, most notably the theories of Jean Piaget and Lev Vygotsky, who have long been engaged in attempting to understand how people make sense of the world around them. Baumann first discusses Piaget's approach, which emphasizes the inherent curiosity of children who tend to develop crude hypotheses that become more complex as they engage in further experimentation. He believes Piaget would see worldview development as an individual and active process, which is a confrontational dynamic necessary for orienting ourselves to our world. As a result, a Piagetian perspective emphasizes a sense of disequilibrium that motivates an individual to resolve or alleviate the conflict, thus bit by bit forming a worldview.

In contrast, Vygotsky's views emphasize the social activities and interactions a person experiences with those more competent and knowledgeable about the world. Baumann explains that the move from data beliefs to control beliefs describes Vygotsky's notion of internalization. The process resembles Piaget's cognitive development approach but emphasizing instead the tools used to mediate or resolve conflicts come from the resources within the person's social or cultural relationships.

Baumann references both Piaget and Vygotsky to highlight the passive (or receptive) and the active natures of worldview development. He sums up by stating:

> All people possess a worldview; its development begins at birth through our primarily receptive interaction with the social environment. While we are active agents that initiate interaction with the world (as indicated by Piaget), the resolutions of these interactions tend to be structured for us by the cultural context into which we are born (as emphasized by Vygotsky). (2011, p. 15)

What then accounts for a change in a person's worldview as he or she ages? Early models of human development gave the impression that psychological maturity was largely complete by adulthood. However, current theories are exploring the notion that worldviews continue to develop throughout the lifespan (e.g., Schlitz, Vieten, & Erickson-Freeman, 2011). Schlitz and her colleagues explore these transformations, which they describe as "a fundamental shift in perspective that results in long-lasting changes in people's sense of self, perception of relationship to the world around them, and way of being" (Schlitz et al., 2010, pp. 19-20). Their work extends from Schlitz's original work with the Institute of Noetic Sciences on developing a non-linear model of worldview transformation. Schlitz illustrates this with a quote from one of her interview participants: "A transformation in consciousness affects a kind of double vision in people. They see more than one reality at the same time, which gives a depth to both their experience and to their response to the experience" (2007, p. 14).

Schlitz notes in several of her works a distinction between minor and major changes in worldview. She explains that the latter is relatively rare and involves a complex reorganization of conceptual structures, both in the features of such structures and how they compare to different conceptual structures. These changes tend to occur within normal processes of psychological development/maturation as people grow in knowledge and experience. Hiebert (2008) also acknowledges these types of changes, describing them as incremental worldview shifts that usually occur in response to cultural changes at the surface level. Examples of these includes advances in medicine that can change how people view the threat of disease or innovative technologies that put people in touch with previously unknown cultures. However, both Schlitz and Hiebert point out that major changes in worldview involve deeper epistemological shifts as well as who people understands themselves to be at an ontological level. These are the kinds of transformations Kennedy and Humphreys (1994) observe in mutual help groups.

The following steps in Schlitz's Worldview Transformation Model (also called the Consciousness Transformation Model) are a result of her work with the Institute of Noetic Sciences, which she develops further in subsequent research (cf. Schlitz, Vieten, & Erickson-Freeman, 2011; Schlitz et al., 2010):

1. Give attention toward greater self-awareness. Danger = deny these experiences.
2. Explore with intention; begin forming an inner compass with which to navigate and make more conscious life choices. Danger = fall into a pattern of continual seeking without making commitments.
3. Practice repetition of new behaviors and the building of new habits. Danger = Practice becomes an end rather than a means.
4. Integrate practice into everyday life; a way of living with new patterns and behaviors. Danger = practices become all about me.
5. Moving from I to We. A desire arises to work actively toward the transformation of my community. Altruism and compassion born of shared destiny rather than duty or obligation can emerge here. Danger = backsliding to being all about me.
6. Living deeply. Engaging in relationships to experience healing, forgiveness, and compassion; growing in wisdom.
7. Bring my new worldview into community; work with others to co-create or shape the social environment and experience collective transformation.

Schlitz and her colleagues (2007) note that transformational practices do not always work in linear, goal-oriented ways that educators may be accustomed to in modern curriculum design. Instead, they assert such practices often work indirectly; they create conditions whereby natural processes of awakening and growth take place. Overall, the worldview transformation model presented here is unique among all literature reviewed for this book and provides a helpful resource for comparison to the theoretical coding that emerged in this research.

Subject Areas Most Related to Worldview Formation

One may presume that an abundance of material on Christian worldview would focus on biblical or theological studies; however, this is not the case. The preponderance of literature focuses on pedagogical factors and strategies for worldview development related to values or moral education and ethics. This suggests a stronger conceptualization of worldview as a manner of living in the world (i.e., the "walking" metaphor) among educators. For example, Carr and Mitchell (2007) argue that discussing values, virtues, or character education only makes sense if teachers and students recognize the prior influence of worldviews or philosophies. They lament a shift seen in Australia away from moral and character education to an emphasis on quality teaching perceived only as a technical enterprise. The authors cite Masters (2003), who defines teaching as simply the application of expert knowledge and skill that achieves improved student learning outcomes. The authors say approaches like these marginalize the development of morality, character, spirituality, wisdom, and wonder in the pedagogical agenda.

Similar to worldview formation, Thomas points out that educating for moral development also seeks "to understand how the moral self attains a state of coherence (internal agreement) and what the relevant factors were that led to such a reality" (2014, p. 31). The author explains that scholars explore these issues so they can establish better programs and pedagogical approaches that produce the morality in students that society desires.

Other teachers use a pedagogy for ethics and values that includes critiquing culture and morality from a Christian perspective (Barron, 2010; Collier & Dowson, 2008; Danaher, 2009; R. Meyer, 2003). This approach complements the study of character and leadership because the two are considered mutually dependent. Thus, leadership and values education are a foundation for decision-making and worldview (Darko, 2009; Fowler, Dickens, & Beech, n.d.).

Carr and Mitchell (2007) tie their emphasis on worldview and values to pedagogy employed in English literature courses, given that the subject is a natural point of departure for examining worldviews. Their students spend time examining a range of texts where human behavior is set within interpersonal, familial, and societal contexts. Their purpose is to have students delve deep into the text to discover the basis for the worldviews observed. They believe these exercises equip students to make more informed decisions and judgments about their own values, which will strengthen commitment to those values in times of hardship and pressure.

Other subject areas that touch on worldview development include diversity, globalization, and citizenship (Carr & Mitchell, 2007; Jordan et al., 2008; N. L. Smith, 2013). Common themes for pedagogical design here include linking curriculum to students' experience and culture, collective learning assignments, in-class debates about moral dilemmas, and using concrete stimuli to illustrate abstract concepts. The learning goals revolve around empathy, tolerance, critical thinking, and global awareness.

The field of psychology is also represented in the pedagogical literature. Many writers acknowledge that human cognition and behavior are powerfully influenced by the worldview construct. For example, Koltko-Rivera (2004) explores its implications to teaching psychological theories of personality, cognition, education, culture and conflict, faith and coping, and even war and peace. He observes that worldview formation lacks in-depth research and theoretical formation within psychology and recommends key areas of investigation including the roles of early caretakers, social institutions (e.g., education and religion), cultural standard-bearers, cultural outsiders, and crucial events over the life span.

The Belief Characteristics of Teachers and Students

The literature shows that teachers play a significant role in influencing the worldview students adopt and how they learn to adapt it over time (Darko, 2009; Fyock, 2008; Wolf, 2011). Andersen (1996) suggests the very nature of the teacher's role will carry this influence despite the desire of the teacher or students. In fact, Schlitz and her colleagues insist the role of the teacher should be given more attention because the classroom community forms according to the example of the teacher who "models coming into an awareness of how to listen for the value of each person's perspective and dialogue across difference" (Schlitz, Vieten, Miller, et al., 2011, para. 43). When teachers and students communicate authentically about worldview issues it can redefine students' direction and growth. Andersen (1996) refers to these as "transforming spiritual moments" and teachers must take the responsibility of being a positive change agent. Fong (2009) agrees seeing her faculty role as a social responsibility rooted in the biblical image of sanctification and toil.

Other influential characteristics include the teacher's ability to integrate Scripture into the subject matter, role-modeling and mentoring students in faith, and genuine Christian conduct in daily life. Teachers have also found ways to apply a religious perspective in the public school system by drawing appropriate attention to character development, particularly moral virtues, which finds common ground in the diversity of school environments (Glanzer & Talbert, 2005). Overall, the literature confirms that a teacher's genuine example is one of the most crucial factors in transforming students' attitudes and behaviors. The teacher is considered an expert due to his or her own experiences in worldview exploration and commitment (Ter Avest et al., 2012).

However, some survey data suggest this influence is not always positive, indicating that teachers do vary in the strength of their commitments to a Christian worldview (Brickhill, 2010; Wood, 2008). Data taken from graduating students in some Christian schools show faculty have done little to reframe their students' engagement with culture, which has allowed voices of humanism and socialism to have stronger influence. Wood (2008) suggests that schools that require faculty to subscribe to a more robust theological position than those who only define a shorter, general statement of faith would see a stronger commitment to teaching a biblical Christian worldview. However, Collier (2013) cautions teachers to ensure their instructional processes do not smack of indoctrination because a school is not a church. Specifically, it is not a platform for preaching a strong Christian message of obedience or conformity. He encourages teachers to allow students space to think critically. Teachers who approach education dogmatically risk ethical contraventions in terms of abusing the power gap between themselves and students.

Walker (2004) argues that increasing diversity and globalization require teachers to develop intercultural competencies. Certainly, this is a primary issue for teachers who work cross-culturally; however, cultural intelligence is becoming necessary for everyone because boundaries and interconnectedness between countries are more fluid than ever. As a result, the worldviews of some students may stand in contrast to the worldviews of teachers raised and educated within a Western society. For example, Walker (2004) describes the challenges faced by educators who work in traditional Arab school settings that face issues of violence between students or toward teachers because the cultural context has normalized such behavior. Teachers who work cross-culturally would benefit from reviewing material from the GLOBE Studies (House, Hanges, Javidan, Dorfman, & Gupta, 2004) that generated abundant data on the relationship between culture and leadership. Given that teaching has strong images of leadership for many people, this project helps with increasing our understanding of cross-cultural interactions and the impact of culture on leadership effectiveness.

As for students, researchers cite surveys indicating that many church-attending youth and young adults hold distinctly non-biblical perspectives. Examples include a rejection of the existence of absolute truth, inability to see the relevance of faith outside of church attendance, viewing core biblical teachings as outdated or wrong, and high percentages of teens who stop attending church after high school graduation (Abshier, 2006; Brickhill, 2010). Other confusing areas for students include the nature of morality, knowledge, and truth when determining moral absolutes, especially when they realize that credible authority figures do not agree on these matters. As a result, students begin to consider absolutes to be the exception rather than the rule (R. Meyer, 2003; Setran & Kiesling, 2013).

Acree (2003) warns teachers not to make unwarranted assumptions about students' thinking processes, especially related to the influence of postmodernity. She states that students do not automatically see contradictions between biblical values and secular theories. Instead, they appear to take a piecemeal approach—viewing biblical values as just one of many approaches to a subject matter and not necessarily the true or preferred one. Therefore, teachers should assume the piecemeal approach to be the norm and include pedagogical practices that push students to confront inconsistencies.

Ter Avest (2012) recommends that teachers take advantage of the natural tendency of adolescents to engage in risky behavior to provoke them to think deeply about religious and secular answers to existential questions. Her focus is on brain development, identity development theory, and the place of critical thinking in worldview formation. She points to research that shows that the developmental stage of certain parts of the brain in puberty and early adolescence might hinder students in managing the consequences of their actions. For example, college-aged students that are just leaving home are especially vulnerable as they explore alternative ways of thinking and living. As a result, Ter Avest claims that students have a natural need for risky behavior and recommends what she calls a *provocative pedagogy* that openly deals with issues related to identity development in both a challenging and caring approach.

Cooling (1994) argues for a similar approach, claiming that teenagers invariably go through a stage of bafflement where they struggle to relate what they know about Christian faith with their emerging understanding of the world, particularly the presence of pain and evil. Collier warns that a pedagogy which "closes down discussion by glib and formulaic answers, may very well lead to a faith cessation or to a retreat into fundamentalism, where the real world is kept at bay by an ideological enclosure" (2013, p. 6). As a result, effective pedagogy must give students space to wrestle with such problems with an open posture.

Overall, teachers in Christian schools should acknowledge that several factors might play a stronger influence on students' worldview development than formal learning. These include the type of school attended for compulsory education, church involvement, personal faith commitment, and parental modeling of genuine faith (Brickhill, 2010).

Instructional and Assessment Strategies in the Field

Pedagogical goals

Borrowing from Cobern's (1996) warfare metaphors, worldview pedagogy activities can be considered tactical devices used to reach small-scale objectives (e.g., sound doctrine, biblical ethics and morality, etc.) within a strategic framework for reaching the large-scale objective of faithful Christian life and ministry. The most common pedagogical goal observed in the literature is raising worldview consciousness. The ability to recognize and respect the logic and moral foundations behind personal perspectives is necessary for the skills that foster collaborative learning, personal prioritizing, and decision-making (Jordan et al., 2008; Schutte, 2008).

Holistic learning appears in the worldview literature, usually in response to the dangers of compartmentalized learning. For example, Setran et al., (2010) point back to the influence of the positivist ideal that separates facts from values. Such ideas allowed faculty to transfer spiritual formation or life application to those outside the classroom while they concentrated on pure academic instruction. The authors posit a rationale for pedagogy that facilitates students' connection of the analytical side of learning with the applied aspects of worldview. While many teachers espouse this pedagogical principle, additional factors such as school culture, resource constraints, or fear of losing academic rigor can diminish its actual pedagogical practice. Setran and his colleagues warn that failing to take full advantage of worldview pedagogy will weaken the formative potential of students' college years.

Finally, Daniels et al., (2000) advocate a liberating goal for Christian worldview pedagogy by claiming it brings much more meaning to life and provides better ways to evaluate success. While their goal is to counter an overemphasis on materialism, they point out that material gains can come as by-products to broader, transcendent priorities.

Transformational learning

Recent models of pedagogy have arisen to counter the limitations of what some writers call the *transmissional* model, which typically features passive, theoretical transmission of information directly to students who respond with mostly independent assignments. Collier and Dowson (2008) examine the pedagogical limitations of this model in the context of a K-12 Christian school that is having difficulty in transforming students' attitudes and behaviors. Their criticisms of transmissional pedagogy include a lack of participatory exploration, the failure to address the underlying values already within students, and inability to equip students for applying knowledge across different contexts.

The authors explore the school's attempt at an alternative pedagogical approach they call a *transformational* model. The hope is to gain active participation from students in the processes of belief and values education. The pedagogical design links a Christian ethical framework to issues in popular culture, thereby allowing students to critique culture from the perspective of a Christian worldview. The strategy features components such as cognitive scaffolding, debating popular culture and relevant moral or ethical issues, practical service learning, and strategic partnerships with local churches. The model was at its initial stages of implementation at the time of the authors' writing. As of 2015, Collier and Dowson have yet to publish further research that evaluates the outcomes of this approach.

Critical pedagogy

Teachers use this educational philosophy to analyze world events, controversial issues, and diversity in hopes of leading students into a vision for better world and social change (Cohen & Gelbrich, 1999). vanSpronsen (2011) uses this approach in his research into student resistance at a Christian school experiencing conflict, which is believed to be the result of a gap between attitudes and behaviors. He cites Bartolomé (2007) who describes critical pedagogy as typically concerned with theories and practices that encourage both students and teachers to understand the interconnecting relationship between ideology, power, and culture. H insists the formation of worldview "not only impacts the attitudes, behaviors, and motivations of students, it also impacts how these are interpreted and understood by the broader school community" (vanSpronsen, 2011, p. 4), especially during conflict with authority figures. The pedagogical approach has considerable merit given that critical pedagogy, at its heart, sees education as an instrument of change for transforming the world into a better place.

Constructivism

The constructivist approach believes that students excel through building new knowledge upon existing knowledge as they interact with the subject matter and their environment. Constructivist pedagogies attempt to identify the issues around which students actively construct meaning. This approach keeps students engaged, generates creativity, and achieves a deeper understanding of the content. It is a popular approach in philosophy and educational disciplines. In fact, Lee (2010) has edited a volume that deals specifically with the use of constructivism in faith-based educational environments.

Danaher (2009) reports on his use of a constructivist pedagogy in a Christian ethics course, making connections to worldview in keeping with the broader literature that acknowledges ethics as a key element in worldview formation (e.g., Brickhill, 2010; Daniels et al., 2000). He chose a constructivist approach due to feedback from students who requested more active learning, customizable assignments, and engagement with issues relevant to their roles as clergy. Danaher used three variants of this pedagogy—learner-centered, inquiry guided, and problem-based—with teaching strategies that featured more dialogue, open-ended questions, and exploration of applied ethical issues. The author reports that students responded to this approach with greater levels of creativity, depth, and breadth not found in traditional modes of pedagogy.

Mittwede (2013) takes a more abstract and technical approach by exploring subsumption and schema theories, especially those popularized by David Ausubel (1960) and Richard Anderson (1977). These provide helpful frameworks for understanding how people incorporate new knowledge into their cognitive structures. His purpose is to explain how worldview transformation can occur through theological education as a type of "remodeling that renews the vision of the learner-disciple in such a way that informs and directs concrete actions in real life" (2013, p. 316). Mittwede addresses a key problem of worldview-level change, which he describes as the "knowledge dump" view of instruction characterized by staid lecture methods. The author describes his attempts to incorporate these subsumption and schema theories, portraying a constructivist approach suitable to worldview formation characterized by an emphasis on classroom discussion, interpretive interaction with texts, and active learning through presentation projects.

Overall, educators should take note of Danaher's recommendation that while constructivist learning is possible for all classes it is likely more effective in smaller ones because these allow for an individualized touch and judgement while students wrestle with the nuances of Christian ethics.

Experiential and social learning

Jordan, et al., (2008) provide a thorough design for pedagogy that prepares students for communal debates about complex and controversial issues in an environment where worldviews vary among different stakeholders. While the authors' context is the field of agroecology, their study has relevance for this research because of its transferrable pedagogical practices. This approach trains students to examine individual and collective worldviews and mindsets critically while at the same time respond to innovative changes occurring in their environment. The authors use experiential learning within group exercises that require students to create a systemic analysis of alternative scenarios for future planning. As students reflect on and experience the social learning required for group debates, the pedagogy focuses on three levels of cognitive processing: cognition, meta-cognition, and epistemic cognition. Each is involved in solving problems, working with tensions, and planning for future development. A key outcome is students learning how to appreciate, challenge appropriately, and change prevailing worldviews in themselves and others.

Jordan, et al., report that their most effective teaching strategies includes: a) the use of concrete stimuli, like evocative photography, to trigger emotional aspects of individual values, b) exercises that require articulating the worldview of another person, and c) group debriefings on common reading resources. The pedagogical goal is to immerse students in complex issues and problems rooted in worldviews. As students learn to understand others, they also learn how to work together toward solutions. This is a valuable approach for use in theological, moral, and ethical debates around Christian issues where worldviews also vary among differing stakeholders.

An important addition to the literature is D. I. Smith and J. K. A. Smith's (2011) edited volume featuring chapters from several university professors who describe their efforts to incorporate historic Christian practices into their pedagogical strategies. The contributing authors reflect on how experiential practices such as hospitality, fellowship, testimony, sharing a meal, time keeping, and adhering to a liturgical calendar enhance their instructional design in college courses across a variety of disciplines. The unifying theme to the book is a search for ways to reimagine teaching and learning in a Christian environment that does not just transfer information but actively engages students' worldview formation in all things toward God's purposes. Three distinct pedagogical models emerge from this book: supplemental, sacrificing, and synergizing approaches. In the first, teachers concentrate on supplementing traditional academic pedagogy with complementary Christian practices. In the second, the attention turns to sacrificing from current teaching habits to prepare students better for formational engagement. Finally, the third model sees pedagogy synergizing academic and Christian practice standards to produce an effect far greater than the individual parts.

Program design for professional studies

The National Institute for Christian Education (NICE) provides postgraduate training in teacher education in Australia. NICE affirms as a best practice the awareness and use of knowledge based on a wide variety of worldview positions because teachers encounter the same realities at other tertiary institutions. NICE requires all students to complete two core units of study that acquaints them with foundational literature from which a Christian worldview perspective is derived. The units also review the nature and role of worldviews along with their role in education.

Fowler, Dickens, and Beech (n.d.) drafted a helpful position paper for NICE that criticizes dogmatic assumptions about the superiority of educational ideas and practices endorsed only by a Christian authority, or by any other single authority, as an example of poor scholarship. Their leadership track encourages students to critique assertions that coherence is achieved through a biblical worldview, which helps identify inconsistencies in applying this worldview to educational leadership. The key themes they look for include servant leadership, accountability, nurture, supervision, example, and vision setting.

A challenge to teaching professional studies within a Christian worldview is that these disciplines do not have a distinctly Christian language or knowledge base. Grauf-Grounds and her colleagues (2009) report on the program design used in a Marriage and Family Therapy (MFT) program situated within a Christian university. The goal was to create a pedagogy that is both faithful to a broad Christian worldview as well as MFT professional standards. The authors believe it is at the worldview level where professional therapists must compare and work with the basic tenets of various belief systems and disciplines.

A person needs a systemic or universal mindset to accomplish this objective because of the holistic assumptions (i.e., theological, professional, and social) that have reciprocal influence on the students' total development. The authors use a working narrative or rubric termed the "ORCA Stance" as a way of articulating their dual goal. It is an acronym based on the components of openness, respect, curiosity, and accountability. The components represent key qualities of both the professional training and Christian commitments the program wants to express. Its brand appeals to all constituents including the university, department, faculty, and students. As a result, mutual commitment to this framework is the starting point for training and pedagogical choices.

Overall, the authors believe professional programs based within Christian institutions would benefit from first developing intentional language that suits professional competencies and standards as well as faithfulness to their Christian perspectives. Pedagogical methods then reinforce the brand and the narrative or rubric provides a way to assess effectiveness of instruction.

Wolf (2011) also addresses this in the context of counselling programs by giving attention to the difficulties professors face in developing foundational life assumptions that undergird the work of the Christian counselor. She describes the frustrations many feel about the oversimplification and lack of theological coherence that can occur when studying a professional program in a faith-based environment. To illustrate, she quotes Poe who also complained that "just add Jesus and stir" (2004, p. 14) is an utterly inadequate recipe for the development of a Christian mind. These types of programs tend to have a curriculum grounded in scientific knowledge and in the writings of established theorists, but integration

33

with matters of faith is too often a short add-on to material. The challenge is understandable given that graduates often require state or provincial licensure and rely on these programs to meet standards for content and ethics.

Wolf's primary concern is the influence of naturalism in professional studies because this worldview seeks to understand its realm on scientific footings without recourse for spiritual or supernatural explanations. Given that these studies are rooted in the philosophical and methodological assumptions of the social sciences, professional programs tend to rely on principles that account for natural phenomena and human behavior as part of the natural world. In sum, Wolf's concern is that teachers overlook theological truths in favor of social scientific understandings of the human condition, which leaves considerations of God's activity with the natural world neglected.

Therefore, according to Wolf, teachers of professional programs who want to integrate Christian worldview must push students to look beyond presented findings to see how the authors arrive at their conclusions and consider what might be absent in the presumptions and methodology. She suggests the use of a heuristic pedagogy in which teachers use methods that guide investigation and enable the students to discover or learn something for themselves. Her examples include: a) providing mental and intuitive triggers so students can ponder how the material relates to a Christian worldview, b) revealing areas in the content that require further study due to unanswered questions about worldview compatibility and then determining how to pursue answers, and c) pushing students into the upper levels of cognitive learning such as synthesis, which requires combining new knowledge with existing knowledge to form original, creative ideas.

A final reminder from Wolf involves the importance of developing caring relationships with students to first earn the trust needed "to address essential issues of spirituality and theology along with other worldview matters" (2011, p. 336). This reflects Noddings' (2013) material on the ethics of care, which seeks to ensure that teachers are completely present with students without showing favoritism. Overall, the teacher's example of care models a crucial part of a Christian worldview worth nurturing in the student.

Instruments for assessment

Three prominent methods of assessing worldview development appear in the literature. First, there is the use of propositional surveys. Morales (2013) lists the following surveys in use by colleges and universities: a) PEERS Test, (Nehemiah Institute, Inc., 2012), b) PEERS II Test II: Christianity and Culture Assessment (Nehemiah Institute, Inc., 2006), c) Creationist Worldview Test (Deckard, 1998), d) Worldview Weekend Test (Howse, n.d), and e) Biblical Life Outlook Scale (Bryant, 2008). The PEERS survey is especially prevalent in the literature. The test reflects an individual's Christian worldview position in five areas, which forms its acronym: politics, economics, education, religion, and social issues. Its primary value is measuring how a person's worldview translates into action, ranking it according to one of four categories of worldview: biblical theistic, moderate Christian, secular humanist, and socialist. Morales does point out that at the time of her research, only a few of these surveys have been tested for validity and reliability.

Second, qualitative feedback from student course evaluations provide valuable data on pedagogical practice (Danaher, 2009; Jordan et al., 2008). Assessment areas that have the most importance for students include connecting worldview issues to real life, empowerment and preparation for vocational issues, suitable levels of active or participatory learning, and quality of connection with classmates throughout the process.

Finally, multi-dimensional surveys are used to explore a person's response to propositional statements, behavioral aspects, and heart-orientation (Naugle, 2004; Schultz & Swezey, 2013). At the time of her research, Morales discovered that few valid and reliable worldview instruments were available to colleges and universities, and most attempt to measure just one or two dimensions of a person's worldview. However, Schultz (2013) recently stepped forward with a new assessment tool, the *Three-Dimensional Worldview Survey* (3DWS), which incorporates all three dimensions. Morales (2013) subjected the 3DWS to principal component analysis and internal consistency formulas and found the instrument to have good construct validity and internal reliability. Thus, educators appear to have a worthy option for worldview assessment with Schultz's 3DWS instrument.

Gaps in the Literature

Electronic databases such as Academic Search Premier and Education Research Complete, as well as web searches using Google Scholar, produced a respectable amount of peer-reviewed literature for keyword searches such as Christian worldview, pedagogy, worldview development, and worldview formation. Further investigation into reference lists led to the discovery of several important books that also address the worldview formation process and teaching insights.

There appears to be far more literature published for the Christian K-12 context on this subject, especially as it relates to values and ethics education. Only emerging qualitative data exist for pedagogical practices in undergraduate education and even less for graduate-level students. This is concerning because many of those Christian institutions promote their curriculum and ethos as situated within a Christian worldview. Although D. I. Smith and J. K. A. Smith (2011) make an important and unique contribution, their book is more experimental and reflective rather than grounded in research. In addition, the conceptualization of worldview throughout the book relies heavily on the Reformed tradition approach.

Most of the literature appears in education-related journals, with only a few articles published in theological journals and religion journals. Unfortunately, no recurring primary authors, practitioners, or theorists appear in the literature on worldview pedagogy. In fact, some of the most focused insights occur in recent doctoral dissertations. Some authors have yet to publish potentially helpful studies mentioned in this literature review (e.g., Belcher, 2009; Collier & Dowson, 2008), which is unfortunate considering their initial articles are over five years old at the time of this review. The most developed pedagogical approach appears to come from Jordan and his colleagues (2008), with its strategic use of experiential learning, cognitive processing, and group problem solving.

Summary and Conclusion

Several disciplines recognize that a person's worldview holds powerful influence over the learning process. Despite philosophical debates among scholars about the construct's usefulness and shifting logic, educators continue to find teaching for worldview formation valuable. Its role becomes real and personal in the lives of students when they wrestle with the implications for their values, ethics, and moral dilemmas. Moreover, teaching students how to discern and interact respectfully with each other's perspectives fulfills the notion of worldview as a holistic reality rather than focusing solely on the propositions a person believes.

Recent models of pedagogy presented here demonstrate a trend in moving away from the transmissional model that relies heavily on cognitive and theoretical instruction coupled with lectures, individual assignments, and research papers. While this model is considered fitting for some purposes, other areas of worldview formation appear to benefit more from a pedagogy that involves social interaction, debating ethics and morality, and systems learning. This type of pedagogy would especially suit Christian traditions that conceive worldview more as a way of living in the world.

Perhaps pedagogies that are more transformational can emerge to meet this need. Teaching of this nature has been addressed for the adult learning context (e.g., Armstrong & McMahon, 2000, September; Brooks, 2000; Taylor, 2009) and others are beginning to articulate a clear theological vision upon which to base its pedagogical planning (Dunaway, 2005). Additional cues can come from the literature on transformational leadership. Bass (1985), for example, proposed four components built on the premise that such leadership engages with others and creates a connection that raises the level of motivation and morality in both the leader and the follower. The following is an adaptation of his construct for the pedagogical relationship (Lindemann, 2012):

- Idealized influence—the degree to which the teacher behaves in admirable ways and displays worldview convictions that cause students to identify with the teacher as a role model.

- Inspirational motivation—the degree to which the teacher articulates a vision of the Christian worldview that is appealing and inspires students with optimism about future goals and meaning for the current situations at hand.

- Intellectual stimulation—the degree to which pedagogical approaches challenge worldview assumptions and stimulate creativity in students to develop innovative ways of problem solving.

- Individualized consideration—the degree to which the teacher attends to individual students' needs and designs coursework with personally meaningful projects that help students grow.

Christian worldview pedagogy of this nature appears to be in the emerging phase. More experimentation and publication of approaches need to emerge that advance this body of knowledge. Considering the significance of worldviews for sound thinking and living, educators in Christian institutions can use this knowledge to create powerful pedagogical experiences.

3

Research Methodology

Introduction

THIS STUDY IS QUALITATIVE research in a grounded theory model using personal interviews with expert teachers in Bible colleges. This approach was suitable because it is "the preferred choice when the intent is to generate theory that explains phenomena of interest to the researcher" (Birks & Mills, 2015, p. 17). The aim of this research was to discover and articulate a theoretical explanation for pedagogy that is effective in forming Christian worldview in college students. Parallel discussions have been conducted in the areas of worldview transformation (Hiebert, 2008; Schlitz et al., 2007; Schlitz, Vieten, & Erickson-Freeman, 2011), worldview change (Kennedy & Humphreys, 1994), and attitude change (Koltko-Rivera, 2004). Each held preliminary value for theory development in this research because of their varied and systematic attention to human learning, change, and transformation.

Given that theoretical development for this topic is lacking in the literature and an explanatory theory was the desired outcome, grounded theory was appropriate for this research approach. According to Birks and Mills (2015), three categories of factors influence the quality of a grounded theory study: researcher expertise, methodological congruence, and procedural precision. The following sections clarify the key factors that affected this study according to those categories.

Researcher expertise

I used this opportunity to learn grounded theory through the process of producing a genuine and supervised study in keeping with its design methods. Learning by doing is an experience common to personal and professional life; consequently, developing anxiety over achieving a perfect research design is unhelpful. Even Glaser (1998) suggests that researchers should stop debating approaches to grounded theory and get on with doing it.

Nevertheless, I do possess experiential knowledge in this subject matter and have done a descriptive, exploratory study for my master's degree, which was published in a peer reviewed journal in abridged form (Lindemann, 2008). I also used the previous coursework in my doctoral program to contribute to the content of this study, to leverage the skills necessary to produce academic writing, to demonstrate the capacity to search for appropriate resources, and to manage an independent scholarly project.

Methodological congruence

A major credibility concern in grounded theory study is attaining methodological congruence, which occurs when there is harmony between an individual's personal philosophical position, the stated aims of the research, and the methodological approach the researcher employs to achieve these aims (Birks & Mills, 2015, p. 35). A strong research design follows a paradigm that is congruent with a researcher's beliefs about the nature of reality (Mills, Bonner, & Francis, 2006). This study aligns well with my personal philosophy because the importance of worldview formation sits within the broader church tradition and professional setting to which I belong and serve. This context informs my belief in the importance of forming a Christian worldview and the advantages to doing so in the Bible college environment. In addition, given that I am a lifelong learner studying reliable principles of educational leadership, social science research, and procedures of scholarly inquiry, this study also fits within an understanding and approach of the integration of faith and learning that I personally hold.

The research questions show clear accordance with my personal philosophy and the intentions of a grounded theory approach. In addition, the interview instrument and other data obtained through triangulated sources (i.e., program objectives, syllabi, and assessments of student learning) support the credibility of the finding from various angles.

Procedural precision

Because several writers acknowledge that undertaking grounded theory research is iterative and evolving, identifying where the data and analytical developments will lead the researcher at the beginning of the study is contrary to its nature (Clarke, 2005; Morse, 2009; Urquhart, 2007). However, it is critical to give careful attention and appropriate rigor to the essential methods of grounded theory if researchers desire colleagues to evaluate their work as quality investigation.

There is much debate as to what constitutes a true grounded theory approach as opposed to straightforward descriptive, exploratory research (Charmaz, 2014; Hood, 2010). For this study, I followed Birks and Mills' essential grounded theory methods (2015, p. 13, Figure 1.2) to avoid the appearance of a selective approach, which Hood (2010) criticizes as diluting the tenets of grounded theory. Nevertheless, despite adherence to established grounded theory methodology, the data analysis and subsequent theoretical formation is unique to the individual researcher because their cognitive style is different from that of other researchers. In addition, the outcome of a grounded theory study is not meant to represent the final word on this topic, but simply a theory "that aids understanding and action in the area under investigation" (Heath & Cowley, 2004, p. 149).

The remaining portions of this chapter will explain the details of the setting, sampling strategy, research design and data collection, as well as procedures used for analyzing the data. The chapter will conclude with a description of my role as the researcher, the key ethical issues involved, and the potential contribution of this study to pedagogical theory, practice, and educational policy.

Setting and Context

This study is situated within Christian higher education, particularly institutions that are accredited with ABHE in Canada and the United States. The roots of these institutions go back to the late nineteenth century movements that drove church leaders to form evangelical Bible schools for the training of missionaries and local church ministers. Historians refer to this initiative as the Bible Institute movement.

Efforts to introduce standardization and quality assurance through accreditation evolved these early efforts into the Bible College movement. Hiebert (2005) describes the enduring purpose of these institutions as providing character and spiritual development as well as ministry competence in an environment of academic formation. He believes this holistic approach to human development fills a gap abandoned by the research universities in the past generation or two. Currently, there are more than 1200 Bible schools and colleges in the United States and Canada with approximately 200 being either accredited by or affiliated with ABHE.

Church traditions and their affiliated colleges communicate a worldview through a variety of mediums. Language, speech, and symbols play a predominant role in communicating culture and the worldviews that shape it. People in communities that share strong values also develop informal ways to use gestures, glances, slight changes in tone of voice, and other auxiliary communication devices to alter or emphasize certain messages (Howell & Paris, 2011). A worldview emerges from intentional instruction, cultural tools of communication, and the activities individuals engage in (Krakowski, 2008). An institution teaches its worldview with intentionality, enculturates it through community life, reinforces it through human interaction, and passes it on through symbols and stories.

de Oliveria (2006) points out that failing to communicate Christian worldview with depth and clarity can lead to: a) the loss of mature members due to emphasizing superficial beliefs and behaviors, b) the growth of syncretistic attitudes by neglecting the exploration of deeper worldview beliefs and transformation, and c) miscommunicating the biblical message by failing to understand cross-cultural contexts.

A review of websites from select ABHE accredited Bible colleges revealed two main emphases related to worldview formation in connection to their mission: a) clarifying the church/theological tradition of the school, and b) equipping students for the cultural situation they will enter after college. For example, Summit Pacific College ("Summit Pacific College - About," 2015) prepares students to interact with differing worldviews while remaining committed to a Christian belief system. In fact, they immediately connect this purpose to their general studies program, further university studies, or a productive Christian life.

Grace Bible College ("Grace Bible College - President's Letter," 2013) brings out the importance of values well by stating their purpose is to prepare students for future choices "with God's values and purposes in view." The president supports this further stating, "There is no value-free education, it is all taught from a particular worldview." The president does bring an assumption of hurt in the broader culture, though, claiming the Christian worldview is the only one "which has the solution to ease the pain we see around us."

Boise Bible College ("Boise Bible College - Doctrinal Position," 2014) exemplifies the typical commitment to Scripture observed across all websites. They stress the educational and spiritual values of the Bible as God's Word, stating: "The faculty, staff, and administration believe that what we read in God's Word is precisely what God meant to say, and that we are all called to holy living and submission to Him and His Word."

Each school gives attention to traditional liberal arts subjects integrated with Christian worldview. Moreover, some schools offer cooperative programs with local community colleges thus combining biblical study with professional marketplace programs. As a result, the importance of faith and learning integration is predominant in these program descriptions.

Most colleges feature capstone courses designed to help upper year students transition from the classroom to professional careers or further studies. These tend to be interactive seminars designed to help students reflect on their college and internship experiences but also learn from the experiences of other students and their worldview formation.

Participants and Sampling Strategy

The unit of analysis for this study were active professors identified by a type of purposive sampling known as expert sampling. This is suitable because this was exploratory, qualitative research seeking to glean knowledge from people with a distinct capability. An expert is defined as a person "having, involving, or displaying special skill or knowledge derived from training or experience" (Merriam-Webster, "Expert," 2003). Hattie's research suggests that expert teachers differ from merely experienced teachers in the way they "represent their classrooms, the degree of challenges that they present to students, and most critically, in the depth of processing that their students attain" (2003, p. 15).

Therefore, this approach is appropriate here because it makes explicit the unpublished knowledge, wisdom, and practices of those recognized as having expert judgment (M. Meyer & Booker, 2001). Bain's similar work in *What the Best College Teachers Do* (2004) serves as an inspiration for this application to the Christian higher education context.

A theologically diverse selection of ABHE member colleges were solicited to participate in this study. I pursued nominations from presidents and deans for teachers who fulfilled the following descriptors of an expert in worldview pedagogy based on observations in the literature review:

- Style of teaching results in increased worldview awareness in students;
- Skilled at integrating Christian worldview into their subject matter;
- Effective at creating a learning environment in which students can explore worldview related issues;
- Well-read and knowledgeable in the integration of worldview and higher learning.

Participants who fit this sample profile were contacted for personal interviews. However, I reserved the right to select certain participants only to ensure diversity of theological traditions. The interviews occurred live through a video conferencing service, which provided a familiar and relaxed atmosphere for the participant. Each interview lasted approximately 60 minutes and was transcribed later from the audio recordings. The interviews were semi-structured so that participants had some direction but were also given the opportunity to develop their line of thought. The questions were open-ended with a focus on drawing out these teachers' perceptions of their expertise, how they developed it, and the ways they currently express it. In addition, I also asked questions to assess each teacher's conceptualization of worldview. The questions followed a funnel sequence that started with broad questions, then probing when appropriate, and concluded with closing questions to ensure clarification or commitment. Final comments served as a check for understanding.

Research Design, Data Collection, and Analytical Procedures

Grounded theory was necessary for this study because this approach attempts to build new theoretical explanations for effective worldview pedagogy in Christian higher education. Creswell explains that a theory is an explanation or understanding of something that is a "drawing together, in grounded theory, of theoretical categories that are arrayed to show how the theory works" (2013, p. 85). While the methodology originated in sociology with Glaser and Strauss (1967), it has since been applied to several disciplines with researchers adopting and adapting the methodologies to fit their own disciplinary knowledge base. Birks and Mills (2015) categorize the development of this approach into two generations. The first centers on Glaser and Strauss' work with their students at the University of California, San Francisco (UCSF) School of Nursing. They provided a challenging and supportive environment that eventually birthed the second generation of grounded theorists from among their students, some of whom produced interpretive work on Glaser and Strauss' methodology while others launched out with their own iterations (e.g., Charmaz, 2000, 2014; Clarke, 2005; Bowers and Schatzman, 2009).

One of the most popular grounded theory researchers to emerge recently is Brené Brown, whose research on shame, courage, worth, and vulnerability (2006; 2012) showcases this approach for explaining what is discovered in compelling ways that resonate with the people who read it. She explains that, "Basically, with the type of research I do, I'm a story-catcher. I listen to people's stories and then subject those stories to a rigorous methodology of making sense of them" (Lieberman, 2012). For Brown, stories are data with a soul. Many laypeople, counsellors, clients, and therapists worldwide testify to the credibility of her writings and workshops.

Overall, there are varying nuances to the grounded theory method so it is important for the novice researcher to specify their approach. This study was done in a constructivist method, which Mills et al., (2006) observe initially in the work of Strauss and Corbin (1994; 1998) and later by Charmaz (2000). The defining attribute of this method is the acknowledgment of the researcher's interpretive influence upon the participants' stories in constructing the theory. Constructivist methodology rejects the assumption that reliable theory can only emerge from a neutral, objective external reality in which the researcher's position is quite separate from participants in data collection and analysis (Martin & Gynnild, 2011). In other words, while the researcher is "developing a conceptual analysis of participants' stories there is still a sense of their presence in the final text" (Mills et al., 2006, p. 7).

The data analysis for this project used inductive reasoning because the research was designed to create general theoretical statements based on the participant's feedback. The process of abstraction was more open-ended and exploratory, most notably during the beginning stages of data collection and coding. An inductive approach was used because it provided a way to organize the data in increasingly abstract units of information (Creswell, 2013). The final theoretical framework follows suit with most inductive studies that report a model with three to eight main themes or categories in the findings (D. R. Thomas, 2006). The following purposes that lie behind the general inductive approach resemble grounded theory and other qualitative data analysis methods:

1. To condense extensive and varied raw text data into a brief, summary format.
2. To establish clear links between the research objectives and the summary findings derived from the raw data and to ensure these links are both transparent (able to be demonstrated to others) and defensible (justifiable given the objectives of the research).
3. To develop of model or theory about the underlying structure of experiences or processes which are evident in the text (raw data). (Thomas, 2006, p. 238)

I used the following procedures for inductive analysis of qualitative data from Thomas (2006, p. 242, Table 2), which he adapted from the work of Creswell (2002, p. 266):

1. Initial read through text data = many pages of text.
2. Identify specific segments of information = many segments of text.
3. Label the segments of information to create categories = 30-40 categories.

4. Reduce overlap and redundancy among the categories = 15-20 categories.
5. Create a model incorporating most important categories = 3-8 categories.

Although it was a time consuming and comprehensive process, the main advantage of this systematic and rigorous data collection method was in obtaining rich data from the experiences and knowledge of these expert teachers. However, this research was limited to the conceptualizing and experiences of the participants; therefore the results cannot be generalized to the larger population of educators. Finally, as a researcher and a fellow educator, I took care to minimize inserting bias through both transparent field notes and a disciplined coding process.

I used a constant comparative method during the personal interviews to analyze the data for increasing levels of abstraction. Similarly, using the responsive interviewing model (Rubin & Rubin, 2011) allowed me to start with a first analysis of interviews before continuing so I could adjust my questioning. I also kept field notes to record details of the settings, the time of the school year the interview took place, a general description of the participants, and the overall dynamics of the interview, including its length. Memoing was recorded in the field notes to log emerging patterns of professional practice, factors influencing concepts of worldview in students, and assessment practices. I used these to record my initial thoughts and explanations on these observations. Because a grounded theory approach has no outliers, any data that did not fit the emerging pattern required me to change the theoretical concepts to fit everything in the model.

In keeping with standard practice, the data were separated, sorted, and synthesized through qualitative coding. For Charmaz, coding means "that we attach labels to segments of data that depict what each segment is about. Coding distills data, sorts them, and gives us a handle for making comparisons with other segments of data" (2014, p. 3). The sequence of coding was based on the interview transcripts and began with initial coding, which were the simple verbatim responses from the participants as they described their experiences and approaches. The second stage of coding, called focus coding, grouped common wording from the statements to uncover early themes that were explored further. The final stage, called theoretical coding, is where distinct patterns, unifying or repeating ideas, sensitizing concepts, and themes begin to emerge from the data in keeping with a grounded theory approach (Bowen, 2006). Ryan and Bernard describe themes as "abstract, often fuzzy, constructs which investigators identify before, during, and after data collection" (2003, p. 85). Overall, I followed two propositions widely accepted by grounded theory researchers: a) everything is data, and b) trust and emergence (Brown, 2006; Charmaz, 2014). In other words, if the researcher is diligent in coding the data and listening to participants, the theory will emerge from the data.

Given that this research involved the influence of different theological traditions, I paid close attention to indigenous categories such as denominational distinctives and shared language. In addition to constant comparison procedures, I wrote with detailed and thick description, used member checking for validating the accuracy of the findings (Creswell, 2013), and trianglulated the data by examining program objectives, syllabi from the participants courses, instructional notes, PowerPoint slides, and some student assessment data that relates to worldview.

Researchers must be aware of obstacles that can affect the trustworthiness of their findings because these affect the subsequent discussion and theoretical conclusions. Such obstacles include insufficient preparation for the interviews and data collection, too much flexibility that can make conceptualization difficult, not accounting for problems with data gathering and analysis, and researcher bias or lack of skills in reporting (Poggenpoel & Myburgh, 2005). Precautions for each of these potential obstacles were tracked in my field journal and any concerns were reported to my dissertation chair for counsel.

After conducting the data analysis, I used that information to write a detailed description of the findings and proposed a theoretical framework for addressing my research questions. I then created a visual model to help others understand the theory and processes. The closing chapter of this book elaborates on conclusions that speak to my research questions, reveals any issues I did not anticipate, comments on any perceived limitations of the study, and states my recommendations for further research.

Role of the Researcher and Bracketing

I completed this research as a doctoral student with George Fox University. I am also an academic dean at an accredited Bible college, and thus I participate in teaching and administrative work geared toward Christian worldview formation. As a result, I have an academic and professional interest in this topic given that my role involves facilitating curriculum and faculty development. Therefore, it is my hope that this research will bring benefits to my own teaching as well as the teaching of my colleagues.

Suspending judgement was especially important during the interview and coding process. Bracketing involves the researcher intentionally setting aside his or her own insights as well as what is already known about the subject prior to and throughout the investigation (D. R. Carpenter, 2007). Bracketing strategies are also a means of demonstrating the validity of the data collection and analysis process (Ahern, 1999).

Because I am a fellow Bible college teacher and administrator, as well as an educational researcher, I anticipated temptation to share insights with the faculty I interviewed. Therefore, I applied several bracketing strategies to this study. The first was to acknowledge the relevant items from my background and preconceptions to this topic. Because I have served in Christian ministry for over 20 years as a pastor and educator in the Pentecostal tradition, this background would color my interpretation of what I hear from the interviewees. In addition, my role as an administrator in Christian higher education can bias my interpretation of the data because I do coach and assist faculty in course design and teaching strategies. Therefore, I used constant comparative methods to ensure fit and that conclusions were grounded solely in the data obtained through interviews with the participants.

I have also been influenced by various writers who address this topic and have published an article that reviews the literature on worldview pedagogy (Lindemann, 2012). As a result, I did not mention these biases and experiences so I could be as receptive as possible to how the participants described their views and practices. During the interview and coding, my sole focus was on the interviewees and learning from their expertise. Any follow-up questions or probes were limited and pertinent to strategies or concepts shared by the participant.

Research Ethics

I took measures throughout this study to ensure the professional, personal, and emotional safety of all participants according to the guidelines for safeguarding human participants set out by George Fox University. Following Institutional Review Board (IRB) approval, I sent an email with a letter of consent to the presidents and deans of select colleges explaining the nature of this study and requesting nominations for participants who fit the sample profile. Upon receiving nominations, I emailed potential participants with a letter of consent explaining the purpose, process, and anticipated benefits of this study. I collected signed consent forms from both nominators and participants.

Once the participants agreed, I arranged a scheduled time for personal interviews as well as the means for conducting them (e.g., face to face, video conferencing). The names of all participants were kept confidential and any identifying information was kept off the audio recordings. I gave each participant a signed guarantee to destroy the recordings after three years. Likewise, the transcripts do not contain any identifying information and I used only initials in chapters four and five of this study. My field journal and field notes were kept on my personal computer and backed up to a cloud-based service and separate hard drive, which are all password protected. The audio recordings were transferred to my field notes and deleted immediately from the recording device.

Potential Contribution of the Research

This study has the potential for creating a helpful theoretical framework for professional educators in Bible colleges who seek greater pedagogical effectiveness in shaping the worldviews of their students. Because the formation of a Christian worldview is a common goal of these institutions, a theory for effective pedagogy grounded in proven expertise would be valuable.

This research can also facilitate the sharing of wisdom and knowledge from experts in the field who seek to form Christian worldview in their students. This includes understanding more about the worldview formation process, what to expect of students, how to treat them, and how to assess their progress. The outcomes resemble Bain's (2004) conclusion that effective teaching cannot be measured solely by exam results. It is also evident in the ways a student retains the material to the degree that it influences his or her thoughts, values, and actions.

4

Research Findings

Introduction

THE PURPOSE OF THIS study was to examine concepts and processes that expert teachers consider when educating for Christian worldview formation. A grounded theory design was used to determine a model for effective worldview pedagogy based on the data. This method of qualitative research allowed me to use a constructivist method in forming the theory from data I obtained using personal interviews with the six participants. I am grateful for these nominations because it allowed me to interact with faculty that others deemed especially competent in this form of teaching. As a result, the validity of the data is strengthened beyond my own opinions of competency. The analyses of the interview data helped me explore the following research questions:

1. What instructional designs and pedagogical methods are especially effective for raising worldview awareness and shaping Christian worldview development?

2. How does the worldview of the teacher and his or her relationships with students influence pedagogical effectiveness?

3. How are teachers assessing college students for worldview awareness and development?

An introduction to the participants

The interviews were held between September 28, 2015 and December 14, 2015 with three participants from the United States and three from Canada; each are faculty in ABHE accredited colleges. All nominated participants were males ranging from early 30's to early 60's in age and each had experience teaching in church-related ministry prior to moving into higher education. Table 1 summarizes more specific information with names rendered as initials to maintain confidentiality:

Table 1: Summary of Data on Interview Participants

Participants	Location	Degree	Role	Teaching Area	Teaching Experience
DW	Western Canada	MA	Administrative Faculty	Christianity and Culture	4 years
JK	Western Canada	PhD	Faculty	Biblical Theology	7 years
RS	Eastern U.S.	PhD	Administrative Faculty	Philosophy	23 years
WH	Western Canada	ThD	Administrative Faculty	Intercultural Studies	18 years
BB	Eastern U.S.	MA	Administrative Faculty	History	4 years
DH	Western U.S.	MA	Faculty	Intercultural Studies	9 years

All interviews were conducted via video conferencing services. Each interview began with some informal conversation and a preamble on research ethics. The rapport was quite good through the video conferencing method, which allowed for conversational dynamics and even responsive humor to be expressed. Each interview was kept to the time limit of 60 minutes with five participants speaking from their work office while another participated at home. All participants expressed genuine enjoyment in talking about the subject matter, although they had differing backgrounds and responses to the overall concept of worldview.

Backgrounds and responses to the concept of worldview.

This section is important to include because it illustrates why these participants demonstrate expertise in the eyes of their nominating president or dean. The opening question of the interview allowed me to explore their affective and intellectual responses to the worldview concept as well as their life and educational backgrounds that contributed to their current thinking on this issue.

Both DH and BB grew up as children of missionaries so they learned about worldviews as a way of understanding differences quite early in life. In fact, BB admitted that he used the term often before fully understanding it. DH has also since adopted two children (one from southeastern Europe and another from Africa) in addition to having two of his own biological children. He stated that the processes involved in adoption and then interacting with the children required a great deal of cultural competence. WH served as a missionary for 15 years, so he experienced firsthand the challenges of cross-cultural communication. He realized this had deep connections to the worldviews held by each party and proved to be a significant challenge in his missionary career. Since that time, he has focused on teaching in these areas of Christian higher education.

DW was in pastoral ministry for eight years before moving into higher education. He links worldview to important matters of discipleship, identity formation, and participation because a crucial aspect of mutuality is at play. He explained that worldview is something we both shape and are shaped by—much like our relationship with culture. Likewise, Christians are participants with God in this world at the same time he is influencing, shaping, and directing us. Therefore, to the extent that a Christian is aware this is happening, he or she becomes better equipped to live a life that is meaningful, has clarity, and proceeds in a healthy direction.

An initial theme emerged when I discovered that WF, DW, RS, and JK did not study worldview as a distinct subject, but instead learned about it indirectly within more prominent interdisciplinary subjects such as historical, cultural, and philosophical studies. As a result, worldview formation occurs as a secondary benefit within the study of complementary subjects. JK mentioned that in his preparation for our interview he realized the term "worldview" is rarely used around his school. He was unsure why this is the case. In fact, because of participating in this research he acknowledged that worldview is an extremely important part of his biblical teaching and a positive aspect of his personal life. This confirms many parts of the literature that describe worldview as often unconsciously held beliefs and values.

However, it is at this point where a couple of the participants did mention they held some negative opinions toward the worldview concept. DW dislikes the study of worldview as a distinct subject because it is often treated as something programmable. For example, there is an implicit understanding that Christian educators are expected to instill in students the "correct worldview" because of taking a certain course or program. But, as DW insists, this is an outcome we have little control over. He believes worldview formation has a lot to do with the posture of the teacher and the institution toward learning and students' expression of worldview. Therefore, worldview formation throughout the whole of student experience is much more attractive to him than worldview indoctrination via designated courses. He maintains this as a more open-handed posture rather than a closed-fisted, tightly controlled approach that insists on conformity to some established standard.

RS dislikes worldview discussions because he sees it as analogous to relativism. Given that his background is from the Reformed tradition, this mindset corresponds with the historical literature reviewed for this study (Naugle, 2002). RS believes the primary educational challenge in our day is whether students will accept the existence of objective truth in matters of philosophy, ethics, or morality. He insists the terminology of worldview is inherently flawed because it does little to challenge people to think beyond "Well, you have your worldview, and I have my worldview." As a result, he argues the worldview concept it not as helpful with a person whose presuppositions assume there is no such thing as objective truth that holds all of us accountable. Thus, he argues, disrupting the influence of relativism among students is the greater pedagogical need.

Participants identified the following areas in college studies as closely related to worldview development: identity formation, holistic life and holiness, learning to place our lives into the narrative of God's purposes in the world, exploring the classic questions of philosophy and the basic questions of truth, epistemological debates involving relativism vs. absolute truth, learning to judge history through the lens of their worldview, and the ability to converse more effectively with the larger culture yet still be effective witnesses of the Christian worldview. In addition, the participants identified several items they personally value about the worldview concept, such as growing in Christian maturity, taking ownership of one's beliefs, the development of critical thinking, and the necessity of learning better conversational skills with diverse people groups holding divergent perspectives. A few additional benefits to worldview formation mentioned include the development of better social consciousness, earning credibility with others, practicing empathy, having greater relevance to our world, and setting a healthy trajectory for future decision-making.

Each participant cited important books and authors that helped them become more educated on this subject. The following is an annotated list of both formational texts and current readings mentioned:

- Bloom, A. (1987). *The closing of the American mind*. Simon & Schuster. RS mentioned this book as one of the first to declare that students would soon enter college holding as axiomatic (i.e., self-evident or unquestionable) that there is no such thing as absolute truth.

- Colson, C. & Pearcey, N. (1999). *How now shall we live?* Tyndale House Publishers, Inc.; Schaeffer, F. (1985). *The complete works of Francis A. Schaeffer: A Christian worldview.* WH mentioned these as key formational texts on his understanding of the Christian worldview concept.
- Downing, D. E. D. & Porter, S. E. (Eds). (2009). *Christian worldview and the academic disciplines.* [McMaster Divinity Press]. Pickwick Publications. WH recommends this to students doing classroom presentation on worldview related to academic topics.
- Georges, J. (2014). *The 3D gospel: Ministry in guilt, shame, and fear cultures.* Timē Press. DH uses this as a textbook because it explains the three primary culture types in the world and how Christians can minister effectively across worldviews and cultures.
- Goheen, M. & Bartholemew, C. (2008). *Living at the crossroads: An introduction to Christian worldview.* Baker Academic. WH uses this as a college textbook because it provides a good analysis of how Christians live in the tension between biblical and cultural stories.
- Hoffecker, W. A. (Ed.). (2007). *Revolutions in worldview: Understanding the flow of western thought.* Presbyterian & Reformed Pub Co.; Sire, J. (2004). *Naming the elephant: Worldview as a concept.* Both were mentioned by BB as an important complement to Sire's book *The Universe Next Door.*
- John Paul II (2000). *Fides et ratio: On the relationship between faith and reason: Encyclical letter of John Paul II.* Pauline Books & Media; Saint Augustine (2008). *The Confessions.* Oxford Paperbacks. RS appreciates these books for their perspective on the Christian life as a matter of faith seeking understanding. He says when faith is genuine it wants to understand its object.
- McGrath, A. (2007). *Christianity's dangerous idea.* SPCK Publishing. BB mentioned this book a good example of

individual's right and responsibility to take ownership of their faith and worldview. Ownership was another initial theme that emerged from several interview participants because it was an important teaching objective.

- Sire, J. (1997). *The universe next door. A basic worldview catalog,* 4th ed. BB and JK mentioned as a foundational text and first exposure to the worldview concept, especially its exposition of worldviews other than Christian theism.
- Walsh, B. J. & Middleton, J. R. (2009) *The transforming vision.* IVP Academic. JK mentioned this as an important text in his graduate studies that furthered his understanding of the worldview concept.
- Wells, D. (1999). *Losing our virtue: Why the church must recover its moral vision.* RS referred to this book's claim that just 17% of Americans regard sin as an offense against God. Which means that 83% of the population would be unable to make any sense of Christ's death at all. Therefore, Christian morality and worldview might hold little appeal to a huge amount of the population.
- Wells, R. A. (1989). *History through the eyes of faith.* HarperOne. BB uses this book to teach students about studying the same history as any other student would, but also using an addition lens of Christian faith; i.e., looking at it with a spiritual dimension. He maintains that Wells' observations are an excellent example of putting Christian worldview to use in studying history.

Initial and Focused Coding

Each research question was investigated through coding the transcribed interviews, comparing the triangulation data, and interpreting the data as a researcher and educator. The participants each had unique concepts and stories to share along with many common approaches, which allowed me to judge a point of saturation. The interview instrument (see Appendix A) consisted of six questions: however, I removed question #4 after the third interview because it proved to be redundant to the participants. I used several elaborating questions to explore their comments further. Altogether, the interview structure followed a typical funnel method with probes, clarification comments, and checks for understanding.

The analysis was completed with an inductive process throughout three stages of coding: initial, focused, and theoretical. During the initial coding stage, I highlighted the transcribed interviews to indicate crucial statements related to the research questions. I then borrowed a practice from social media of using hashtags to designate keywords and initial themes, which also allowed me to group them according to initial themes. The hashtags also allowed me to assemble quantitative data using the search feature in my word processor. As a result, I could identify recurring keywords and themes. Constant comparative methods were used throughout the interview process by keeping field notes and inserting footnotes in the transcripts to indicate similarities and difference between concepts, factors, and initial themes.

Focus coding was used to group common wording from the interviews and triangulation data to test for theoretical sensitivities that were explored further in the next stage. The initial portion of this stage produced 93 keywords, which I then searched for statistical tendencies within the transcripts. I reduced overlap and redundancy to produce 19 categories of data, followed with further coding that determined nine prominent relationships among these keywords, which represent the core categories. Given that the methodology for this project did not rely solely on statistical observances, the constructivist approach to grounded theory required me to observe all data like a story-catcher, exploring and interpreting the experiences of the participants where no a priori theories currently exist so new possibilities could emerge and be communicated with soul and vitality (Birks & Mills, 2015)

The remainder of this chapter presents the findings of the interview questions followed by a discussion of the emergent themes discovered through theoretical coding. The chapter concludes with a summary of items that appear consistent with the literature as well as surprises in the findings. Further discussion on the themes and the proposed theory/model for worldview pedagogy are addressed in the next chapter.

Analysis of the Data

Key pedagogical factors to consider

The participants addressed three principal areas: a) issues to clarify in themselves, b) inherent factors to accept in students, and c) cultural and belief factors to confront. A basic issue each had to clarify was whether worldview development was the primary or secondary benefit of the subject matter they were teaching. In fact, only two of the six participants directly address worldview as a subject within their courses; the others provide secondary attention through other subjects. This revealed important assumptions about the nature of worldview formation consistent with the literature; namely, that it takes place implicitly within the context of other pursuits. This paralleled the emphasis on discipleship formation in each school's statements of mission. In other words, it is assumed the entire college experience exists within and contributes, sometimes indirectly, to forming students' Christian worldview. This could account for why institutions are struggling to assess worldview, given the priority to other specific learning outcomes.

Another key factor within teachers arose with respect to clarifying their role and specific passion as educators. For example, DW mentioned that his mindset is based on the pastoral perspective he brings to the college context. He explains as follows:

> If I were to describe the goal or vision of my teaching, it is pastoral teaching. I have always felt I had one foot in the church and one foot in the academy. I still have not discerned which one except to discern that it is neither; it is not a choice. It is a value and benefit to be able to do this, especially in a Christian institution where in

some ways I get to exhibit my pastoral interest, gifts, and strengths while and at the same time push into the academic side. So, I do not feel like I must choose. I do not feel like it was a change in profession to come teach here. The change in context helped me engage this question of worldview and personal formation. (DW, interview, December 14, 2015)

Two participants brought up a fascinating perspective, stating they did not feel their role was to exclusively advocate for their denomination's distinctive interpretations of Scripture or core doctrines. While they were certainly adherents to those positions, they felt it was too pedagogically confining to limit exploration of differing perspectives. Instead, they were driven to contend for the development of critical thinking and greater ownership of faith and worldview by teaching students to come to sound conclusions using appropriate methods/skills in reasoning and hermeneutics. What must be accepted is that these conclusions may differ from other students, teachers, or even the school.

Several factors inherent within students also arose from the data and the participants accepted these as limitations to worldview formation in the college setting. Chief among these are the bounds of personal maturity and cognitive development. Together with general cognitive abilities, these represent the overall readiness and values in students that move the learning process forward. JK contrasted the basic abilities of an 18 to 22-year-old versus mature student in understanding and applying the course material. He observed that life experience and intrinsic motivation increases the depth of processing necessary for worldview formation. In addition, younger students tend to follow cultural and media distractions, which take priority over the life and career-planning concerns of their older classmates.

Students can also set limits to the level of relationship they want to develop with their teachers. WH sees this especially in the informal parts of the college experience. For example, only certain students will follow up with him outside of class with conversations, discussions, or questions. These are vital to their development but it depends on a student's willingness to engage or make the effort to reach out and talk.

Another key factor that arose is that some students simply do not fully engage in their faith and are vulnerable to falling away from Christian belief. This attunes with DW's caution about viewing worldview development something a school or teacher can control. He says one of the main problems is when teachers want to assert too much control it affects their teaching style (i.e., their posture), which may or may not be that inviting to students. In sum, an overly controlling or haughty approach from the teacher often results in negative learning outcomes for students. DW explains there is a huge diversity of expectations among students on the Church's role as an ambassador of the gospel. This mirrors what Kanitz (2005) says about the multiplicity of Christian worldviews. A visual image DW uses to describe contrasting postures from faculty is open hands or closed fists. The former is open to allowing diverse perspectives and the messiness of learning. The latter is less tolerant to such dynamics.

Moreover, these postures are not just individual; an institution also communicates a posture toward things deemed valuable or not as it relates to education and worldview formation.

Finally, there are crucial factors to consider with the influence of contemporary culture and belief patterns in society, which teachers inevitably confront as they address worldview-related areas. A recurring issue arose from the participants concerning the lack of seriousness college-aged students express toward sin and holiness. JK argues these concepts are especially important because of their connection to questions all worldviews address, especially concerning the source of problems in our world (Sire, 2009; Walsh & Middleton, 1984). In fact, RS finds that students do not consider it significant that God forgives sin because their ethical reasoning holds that God should forgive sin because people deserve it. He especially laments the lack of realization among students concerning the cost to atone for sin. This reflects the de facto creed observed in American teenagers described by sociologists Smith and Denton (2005) as moralistic therapeutic deism. The authors found American teenagers to be extremely inarticulate about their religious beliefs, with most unable to offer any serious theological basis for their views. RS suspects that the lack of secondary-level education in morality or ethics for students who have come from a public education background may also contribute this factor.

The participants in this research also expressed great concern over students' general ignorance of the nature and origins of the Bible and their struggles to engage it with critical reflection. WH claims the media-saturated culture among teenagers and young adults distracts them from spending enough time to wrestle with these worldview-related issues and read literature that can challenge their assumptions. However, BB mentioned a key issue that also arose in Schlitz's (2007) work: the attraction to continual searching for truth without making a commitment to it. BB describes a recent student with this tendency:

> I would say he has made the search for truth the end goal. He enjoys asking all the questions but he is not going to be convinced by the answers from any perspective. He just enjoys the search. Well, I like to search for truth too, but I tell my students that the search for truth must lead you to the truth. You actually have to draw a conclusion. (BB, interview, October 14, 2015)

Learning objectives related to worldview

Analysis of the interview and triangulation data revealed five principal areas of learning objectives for worldview development in college students: a) articulation of their beliefs, b) development of critical thinking, c) nurturing a stronger sense of Christian identity, d) respectful interactions with those of differing perspectives, and e) analyzing the nature of truth.

Four of the participants mentioned that an important outcome for a college-level education is the ability to articulate a personal worldview. In fact, WH's school recently adopted new student learning outcomes, one of which states that students will

RESEARCH FINDINGS

develop and deepen their Christian worldview. This was in response to ABHE's newest standards that elevate the concept and require schools to assess how students are acquiring and applying a biblical worldview. WH admitted that previously the school mostly assumed worldview development was happening so they did not verbalize the components a great deal. But now the school tracks all syllabi for attention to worldview issues; i.e., how it is presented and assessed. BB also gives worldview articulation a high priority in his history courses. He is motivated to teach students the language, terminology, and philosophy-related issues so they can effectively describe their worldview as well as that of others—both past and present. He hopes this will equip students to be more relevant to those they encounter throughout life. Overall, the assignments, teaching strategies, and PowerPoint files reviewed for triangulation data revealed several uses of reflection papers, class discussions, and conversation partner strategies all designed to help students articulate the essence of their Christian worldview.

Training critical thinking capacities appeared in all interviews and triangulation data in varying degrees. RS supplied this helpful metaphor to describe his related learning objective: To train their ears to hear. He wants students to become sensitive to poor and fallacious reasoning because if they cannot spot these they will not know how to respond with a more rationale argument. RS explains why the life of the mind is so important:

> Christian life is a matter of faith seeking understanding. Jesus tells us to love God heart, soul, and mind. So, if the mind is not included then I think we are falling short. It seems to be when faith is genuine it wants to understand its object. I like John Paul II's example of the church—it is more beautiful the way he says it—that we rise on two wings. Wings of faith and reason. I do not think it is right to equate them but still reason has a place. (RS, interview, November 4, 2015)

It was clear from these interviews that participants would consider fideism to fall well short of the expectations for college graduates. In fact, DW's school recently started using an

65

assessment tool called the Watson-Glaser™ Critical Thinking Appraisal to bring greater attention to the cognitive abilities relevant to this objective. The instrument is based on three keys to critical thinking summed up as the acronym RED:

- *Recognize assumptions:* Separate fact from opinion.
- *Evaluate arguments:* Impartially evaluate arguments and suspend judgment.
- *Draw conclusions:* Decide your course of action.

Another set of objectives involve developing a more coherent sense of identity. Two of the participants were especially concerned about the separation between beliefs and behaviors observed in their students. JK referred to this as compartmentalization, saying "It is important that students understand that God actually wants to have access to every area of our lives. Being set apart to God is an integral part of our worldview" (JK, interview, November 11, 2015). As a result, the desire to increase students' ownership of their faith and worldview arose as a common learning objective. The participants confirmed the first place of grounding for a Christian worldview is in Scripture with a predominant emphasis on the themes of the Bible, even if the course is designated as a professional or general studies area. In doing so, students are given the tools for continued reliance upon Scripture as a reference point in their lives. The participants agreed that students must learn to take responsibility for intentional faith and worldview development because, while they will not always have an authority figure, like a professor, around to rely on for easy access or accountability, they will have the Bible.

DW describes his goal here as setting students on a sustainable trajectory to engage their worldview and fundamental beliefs. This terminology recognizes that while teachers can do a lot for students in a course or academic program they cannot do it all. Therefore, worldview pedagogy involves mapping out a path for students to move forward as life-long learners, primarily where Christian faith engages complex questions and social issues that challenge the clarity of a person's worldview. This trajectory image is valuable for theory-building because it represents the directional yet evolutionary nature of worldview formation. DW referred again to the image of open hands here to emphasize that attempts to control or finalize the outcome of worldview formation is unhelpful because this development is more of a slow process in a good direction. Admittedly, this is a difficult objective to assess because it involves the intangible task of evaluating a person's sense of identity. As a result, several of the participants rely on observing where students make connections and integrate things they are experiencing into a more coherent worldview. Of course, the primary limitation to assessment is the length of time students choose to spend in college under the observation of their teachers.

Another recurring objective from the data was educating students on interacting with those of differing perspectives and worldviews. BB offered a compelling case by arguing that if his students cannot put themselves in the shoes of historical figures, then how could they show empathy for the past and present. For him, equipping students for credibility and relevance has vital implications for Christian witness and social consciousness. Similarly, teaching empathy appeared in four of the six interviews. However, an examination of the triangulation data did not reveal a consistent emphasis in the syllabi descriptions or assignments. This objective appeared to be more prominent in classroom dynamics and active learning. For example, DW links this to the importance of a teacher's posture, especially in modelling an honest clarity and a humble conviction. He often uses this as a tagline in his classroom teaching when dealing with challenging topics that raise emotions and have potential for conflict. He insists that diluting a worldview just to avoid conflict is unhelpful. Engaging in these topics can be done in ways that foster relationship and invite people to interact. This objective is also observed in the literature, especially by Jordan, Bawden and Bergmann (2008) as well as Schlitz, Vieten, and Miller (2010). The goal appears to be promoting constructive dialogue among groups who share common social interests and concerns but "differ in epistemological, ontological, and/or axiological aspects of their own particular worldviews" (Jordan et al., 2008, p. 93).

Similarly, a key learning objective for DH is preparing students for the exchange of ideas among peers and those outside of their denominational tradition. He supports the observation from Kanitz (2005) who argues that worldview pedagogy can be more effective through examining not only the shared tenets among the various traditions, but also the nature of denominational and institutional differences as well as cultural currents that are influencing today's students. DW insists the way a teacher demonstrates their own engagement in these areas goes a long way to inviting students into social consciousness.

The final learning objective that appeared throughout the interviews involved analyzing the nature of truth. JK put it well by acknowledging that part of his teaching involves convincing students that the worldview of the Bible should be our worldview. He agrees with Estep who states,

> The Bible is the epistemological center of the Christian faith. Without the Bible, theology would become undirected speculation about an elusive God who does not want to be known . . . As for every aspect of the evangelical tradition, the witness of Scripture is of paramount importance. (2008, p. 44)

Half the participants find it a challenge to convince students to accept the existence of absolute truth and dissuade them of the cultural trend toward moral relativism. RS observed that students do have selective acceptance of objective truth, such as with math and science. However, what he tries to show them is that the tenets of relativism not only undermine religion and philosophy, but science as well, because it too is affected by differences in perception, consideration, and political interests.

The situation can be discouraging, as RS admits; however, he suspects that contemporary teachers share more in common with the challenges faced by the early church in presenting the gospel to a pluralist culture. BB is not so discouraged, instead taking comfort in the idea that Qoheleth would still say there is nothing new under the sun (cf. Ecclesiastes 1:9). Likewise, he thinks Plato, Socrates, and Protagoras would recognize the philosophical positions in our contemporary debates because we live with these same types of people right now (i.e., stoics, existentialists, epicureans, etc.). Therefore, it is important that students understand this epistemological big picture, given that they may have an opportunity to share the Christian worldview with any of the groups mentioned above. In doing so, RS explains that relativists are offended at the notion of absolute truth because it implies a person knows it, which is judged as arrogant. But he argues that just as absolute time exists, so also does absolute truth. The problem lies in our abilities to measure it and comprehend it. For example, RS points out that both the atomic clocks used by the naval observatory and Carbon 14 dating have a degree of inherent error, even though it is very tiny. Likewise, we do have to accept similar limitations within a Christian view of absolutes as we seek to comprehend truth.

Instructional designs and pedagogical methods

The data in this area were grouped into principles and practices. I asked the participants about a recurring idea observed in the literature that involves taking students through a disruption phase, sometimes called disequilibrium, with their current worldview so foundational change becomes possible. Wolterstorff (2002) argues in favor of this phase because it kindles curiosity or dissatisfaction with the status quo. However, Belcher (2011) points out that disequilibrium can bring tensions to the surface and lead to diverse declarations of worldview, supporting DW's conviction that worldview development cannot be overly controlled. Belcher also argues that attempts to discourage disequilibrium will cause tensions to go underground and eventually deteriorate the school culture. Schlitz, Vieten, and Erickson-Freeman (2011) report that despite the fact people can point to pivotal moments that catalyze worldview transformation, in retrospect they can often recognize a combination of factors that destabilized their previous worldview and set the stage for change.

This principle was confirmed by DW who articulated it as the deconstruction-reconstruction aspect of Christian higher education. He acknowledges the situation is delicate because of the political tension involved with deconstructing aspects of the denominational tradition that financially supports that college. Nevertheless, this process is necessary because it reflects the historical development of these traditions. DW describes it further:

> We realize that even our confessions of faith took years, decades, and in some cases, centuries to be formulated. So, there is a value in that process and some of that is uncomfortable. So, deconstruction or, as you say, shaking things up, is really valuable, in some ways—and even students have described it as someone throwing a puzzle in the air and you must put the pieces back together . . . So what we emphasize is that you do not have to put the puzzle back together by yourself. You can invite others to help you put the pieces back together and make sense of the disorientation you experience. So that is where we put an emphasis on community and discipleship with others. It is critical to this deconstruction process. (DW, interview, December 14, 2015)

Other participants admitted that deconstruction alone is unhelpful, especially if it is perceived as an annoying tactic, which DW described as one of the ways that teachers can have a negative influence on worldview pedagogy. However, inviting students to reconstruct together can prevent the isolating effects of disorientation. Overall, the key danger with this phase is that students may respond by redoubling efforts to protect themselves from further destabilization.

Only WH did not see this as a key principle in his pedagogy, expressing instead that it seems harder to convince students of the necessity of forming a strong Christian worldview. He suspects the more students are engrained in our secular environment's abundance of media and rapidly changing culture, the less they are paying attention to wrestling with issues that can challenge their presuppositions. This observation, coupled with the notion of disequilibrium, underscores earlier comments on student readiness to engage the process as a crucial pedagogical factor.

Another important principle includes providing a safe environment for the exploration of ideas. Teachers must know how to wisely push boundaries and survey the spectrum of beliefs on certain topics, especially beyond denominational creeds. This is crucial for educating the social skills of students as they seek to honor the convictions of other groups. Both DW and BB recognized they must be conscious of sensitivities that students carry about certain topics and the anxiety exploration may create. They notice that a teacher's empathetic posture invites students to engage despite their struggles.

The participants also shared some important pedagogical practices helpful in worldview formation. These occurred in both the classroom activities and the types of assignments they create. This was also the most helpful area supported by the triangulation data, which consisted of syllabi, PowerPoint slides, discussion guides, and sample papers. For example, four of the interviewees mentioned Socratic methods of teaching as critical for this type of pedagogy. RS commented that the classroom is the place to draw things out in students. "They will make their proposal and I will dig away at it" he says. "I ask 'what do you mean by that?' over and over" (RS, interview, November 4, 2015). The technique is designed to promote conversational exploration of the issues and encourage deeper ownership in the students for their beliefs.

DW believes it is important to first let students explore their thoughts before turning to the theory and textbooks. He wants students to go beyond the like-dislike evaluative binary and truly dig into why they hold the values they do. BB supports, this saying he is not afraid to challenge students or counter their arguments or statements, especially if he thinks it is from a very limited perspective.

Most of the interviewees use conversation partner strategies in the classroom. The topics and instructions were often open-ended to encourage exploration of opinions and learning to listen to one another. It is clear these teachers work hard to create a lively classroom environment full of robust discussion, which reflects the constructivist techniques observed in the literature (cf. Danaher, 2009; Jordan et al., 2008). These methods were followed up with equally vigorous engagement with established knowledge in the topic (e.g., ethics, biblical theology, history, etc.), so students were forced to research, compare, and reflect on their initial positions. In fact, there were many reflection exercises and assignments observed in the triangulation data.

Both DH and DW use field trips in their instructional design to provide relevant cultural engagement. DW is also the director for a unique program in his college that focuses on urban culture and topics surrounding social justice, the arts, and faith in the marketplace. The field trips in this program are designed to raise student awareness of worldview issues as they relate to a rapidly changing culture. Thus, he uses a type of experiential learning, although the theoretical underpinnings of this theory were not highly developed. DH also takes students off campus to visit non-Christian religious sites, such as Buddhist temples, to give students firsthand experiences with diverse beliefs and people groups so they can grow in social consciousness and communication skills. He also highlighted uses of tactile learning, where materials are brought into the classroom so students can touch and handle them as a means of making connections to more abstract concepts of culture and worldview.

The relationship between teachers and students

The literature review demonstrated that the example of the teacher and their relationships with students can redefine the direction and growth of those they instruct. A teacher's ability to model how their worldview is informed by Scripture and how they dialogue across differences with other people sets a powerful example.

The participants responded with a variety of perspectives on being an example of what they hope to teach when elaborating on this portion of the interview. For instance, JK hopes that his way of living as one saturated in Scripture demonstrates the benefits of a Christian worldview. He draws inspiration from Spurgeon's description of John Bunyan: "Why, this man is a living Bible! Prick him anywhere—his blood is Bibline, the very essence of the Bible flows from him. He cannot speak without quoting a text, for his very soul is full of the Word of God" (Spurgeon, 2013, p. 268). However, he is cautious not to share too much about himself as an example because students should look to their own their experience to form their worldview and, of course, the person of Jesus Christ as their ultimate archetype.

DH cautioned that the classroom environment is an unnatural place of relationship and can set things up for misunderstandings. He also mentioned the possibility of a teacher's negative influence here, such as setting a tone of indoctrination by discouraging critical thinking or misusing their position of power with students. To help mitigate these limitations he balances this with more natural relationship time spent outside of the classroom to serve others, socialize, and solve problems together.

RS pointed out that teachers can also have a negative influence on students by trying to meet unrealistic relational expectations. He explained as follows:

> I deny the popular expectation that effectiveness means being everybody's buddy ... When it comes to school activities I try to stay in touch with the students and make them feel welcome but I do not try to be everybody's buddy. There are other people on the staff that are much more outgoing than I am but I do not think it has hurt my ability to deal with a student. (RS, interview, November 4, 2015)

These insights on the potential negative effects of teachers on worldview formation were not observed in the literature. As a result, these data provide an important addition to the writings on worldview pedagogy.

Participants also mentioned the value of letting a student's voice be heard in both classroom and one-on-one meetings. In doing so, a teacher models the skills of mature interaction as another person relates his or her perspective. This is an example of the way teachers influence the social development of students, which experts note as a core capacity for citizenship as it relates to worldview (Jordan, Bawden, & Bergmann, 2008; Schlitz, Vieten, & Miller, 2010). But this should not be confused with simply being polite or amicable. In fact, WH insisted that part of his responsibility includes confronting students on poor behaviour or academic performance. He knows how he conducts these crucial conversations can have as positive an effect on student development as the formal curriculum.

Assessment approaches

The interview data confirm that all the participants' schools have yet to find an effective way to assess worldview in their students. Foremost among the challenges appears to be finding a way to get valid, observable data on such a deep and integrated part of a person's identity. As a result, DW pays attention to students' abilities to make connections and assimilate some of the things they are taught with what they are experiencing. This echoes Hiebert, who says, "At the core of worldview transformations is the human search for coherence between the world as we see it and the world as we experience it" (2008, p. 315). Each participant also reported they have yet to find a workable assessment tool for worldview development. However, none of the participants were familiar with the assessment tools discovered in the literature review such as the PEERS Test (Nehemiah Institute, Inc., 2012) or the 3DWS (Schultz, 2013).

Overall, most schools represented here prefer that students can articulate their worldview rather than answer the right questions on a propositional-oriented inventory. For example, the program directors at JK's college hold year-end interviews with students where one of the questions touches on worldview-related areas and how Bible college has given them a foundation for life and ministry. Another common approach was to use capstone courses for senior students where reflection on worldview development is part of the learning activities. However, despite these efforts each participant admitted they did not know if any of these data were being compiled, analyzed, and tracked over time. In fact, none of the schools had explicit assessment data they could send me as triangulation sources. In general, participants report their colleges are assessing doctrinal, behavioral, and philosophical components of worldview but do not bring them together as clearly as they would like to gain a picture of student worldview development and application. I suggest this is related to the initial theme mentioned earlier of worldview formation as a secondary benefit to studying other subjects.

The practice of assessing by small gains emerged from coding the data. The participants would practice this primarily through formative assessment, summative coursework, and informal interactions with students. RS describes his assessment as piecemeal and incremental; going question by question looking for ways to give feedback to students that affirms development gains and challenges them to further growth and clarity. Both DW and DH acknowledge the moderate size the of their schools helps with a small gains approach because they get to know students better through the varying contexts outside of the classroom. They call these soft or social evaluations. However, they do admit that collecting valid data on this area can be ambiguous for compilation and annual comparisons. Once again, this reflects the secondary benefit theme whereby worldview development is tied to more traditional areas of assessment, such as biblical literacy, ministry skills, writing ability, and critical-thinking capacity.

Emergent Themes

This section reports the outcomes of theoretical coding that emerged at the latent level, which means these four themes represent the underlying ideas and patterns in the data pertinent to the research questions at hand (Boyatzis, 1998).

Preliminary factors related to teachers, the curriculum, and students

A teacher's posture towards learning is communicated, often implicitly, in ways that invite students to engage in worldview formation in positive or negative ways. A positive posture from the teacher involves clarity of biblical principles coupled with a humble conviction that these truths are valid and reliable. Conversely, a negative posture is created when a teacher is overly controlling and disrespectful of diverging opinions or perspectives. This results in a learning environment conducive only to students who share similar life themes and narrow ideologies. A Christian teacher must be clear on the worldview-related goal they are contending for in terms of student learning. Each participant in this research held passion for key components of worldview formation. Examples include, that students accept the existence of objective truth, that they are able to integrate Scripture throughout their lives, that they can place themselves within the mission of God in this world, and that they can articulate their worldview. These components reveal the opportunities for student worldview formation depending on the focus of the subject at hand. Therefore, a key question must be resolved—namely, are worldview issues a primary or secondary focus to the subject matter? In the case of these participants, worldview formation was often secondary in focus, which appears to contribute to the difficulty of assessing its development throughout the curriculum.

Finally, students bring crucial factors to consider as well. Their readiness to engage in formation emerged repeatedly in the data. Students are at various levels of maturity and inclination to get past the distractions and competing ideas of culture so they can apply the critical thinking necessary to make the most of what Schlitz (2007) calls noetic moments. These moments have power to sensitize them to matters of sin and holiness as they root their lives deeper in Christ. College educators only have a limited amount of time with students corresponding with their program. As a result, deeper learning and/or change is not always feasible despite the expectations or marketing messages of Christian higher education.

Relevant and holistic learning objectives

The literature review and data from this research confirm the common cognitive objective of students being able to articulate the primary components of their worldview. In other words, students need to bring prudent biblical and theological knowledge to bear on describing the reason for the hope they have in Christ, which stands in stark contrast to diluted and bewildering positions like moralistic therapeutic deism. As one participant put it, faith that is genuine seeks to understand its object. Faith inspires the holder to greater intellectual comprehension, which equips the learner to discern good reasoning from bad. A recurring affective learning objective is for students to learn empathy, which is the ability to understand and share the feelings or perspectives of another. Empathy has value for the present as well as the past. It fosters gentleness instead of judgement; it values robust discussion without hostility. Finally, the data show that expressions of students' ownership of faith and worldview is foremost among conative objectives. Huitt (1999) describes conation as connecting the cognitive and affective to behavior through its close association with the issue of "why." The student's motivation becomes personal, intentional, planful, deliberate, and goal-oriented. Teachers long for students to become proactive, rather than reactive, in developing their worldview. According to the Oxford Dictionary, the definition of reactive is "acting in response to a situation rather than creating or controlling it" ("Reactive," 2011). If Bible college teachers can tap into proactive motivations, it can help set their students on a sustainable trajectory of stable Christian faith and good discipline (cf. Colossians 2:5).

Student learning is limited by the levels of readiness and cognitive abilities inherent to individual students. The data present worldview development as a slow process, which can be elusive to clear assessment. Moreover, a student's worldview continues to form after leaving college, so Bible college educators should not consider it their duty to produce an end-product or completed point of arrival. As Galindo (1998) points out, students are neither blank slates when they enter the learning environment, nor are they finished products; they have simply moved a bit more on the redemptive process.

The distractions of popular culture persist as the most immediate danger to Christian worldview. The situation demands much more critical thinking than Poe's amusing adage, "Just add Jesus and stir" (2004, p. 14). The challenge involves teaching students to evaluate their world through the filter of guidance provided in Scripture, but also dispel the oversimplified notion that a Christian worldview can be satisfactorily distilled down to a set of correct propositional answers on a doctrinal inventory.

The deconstruction-reconstruction (D-R) continuum and active learning

I use the word continuum here because it illustrates a "continuous series of things that blend into each other so gradually and seamlessly that it is impossible to say where one becomes the next" ("Continuum," 2011). According to one participant, students describe the experience as throwing a puzzle in the air, then rebuilding it. Therefore, student perceptions do feature unsettling moments and times where the pushing of boundaries feels risky. Creating an environment of community participation through active learning methods helps keep students from sliding into isolation as they navigate the continuum. Helpful strategies here include robust discussion and debates, field trips, tactile learning, debriefing on common learning resources, and classroom presentations. Along with these helpful teaching strategies, the professor's example of genuine Christian worldview appears to be the most important relational advantage to enhancing a student's learning experience. In specific, the interview data reveal that a teacher's devotion to Scripture and their ability to integrate its principles into life and pedagogy is as important as the literature suggests (Ter Avest et al., 2012).

College-aged students tend to have limited critical thinking abilities and sometimes inadequate life experience which they can reflect upon for deeper learning. Also, teachers must remember the pace and vitality they bring to deconstruction varies from class to class. Moreover, students' sensitivities to deconstructing experiences should be monitored to avoid excessive discouragement. The data also suggest that a student's initiative or willingness to respond to relationship-building with faculty sets the limits on potential benefits gained here. Examples include informal, follow-up conversations, service-learning together, and receiving admonishment from faculty members.

One danger is worth noting here. Some teachers pride themselves on a pedagogy that creates more questions than settling firm positions. Hiebert challenges such deconstructive practices, claiming "damage might even happen to students at some Bible colleges where professors sometimes tend to leave their students with more questions than useful answers to these questions, all in the name of "university level" education and sometimes out of concerns for responsible advocacy" (2005, p. 45).

Assess for small gains

The data demonstrate an assumption traditionally shared by institutions; namely, that Christian worldview formation happens implicitly within the standard structure of a Bible college curriculum, the exposure to seasoned Christian teachers, and the spiritual ethos of the campus. However, newer requirements to demonstrate how programs enable students to achieve a biblical worldview is challenging faculty members to pinpoint exactly where to assess progress toward and/or achievement of this objective, especially when such development is secondary in emphasis. None of the institutions represented here have found a satisfactory worldview assessment tool. Moreover, multiple choice tests or propositional-focused tools are a less preferred approach than something that demonstrates a student's ability to apply or integrate theological knowledge. As a result, faculty often resort to assessing small academic and personal gains observed in various components of worldview, such as critical thinking, the ability to articulate philosophical tenets, or the application of orthodox doctrine to practical living. The approach seems suitable and faculty appear content to work within the slow process of transformational learning that undoubtedly continues long after graduation.

Summary

The findings reveal several major areas consistent with the literature, such as learning objectives that raise awareness of worldview issues and the desire to see students gain greater ownership of these matters. Teachers want students to become more intentional about evaluating the cultural stories that compete for their attention and devotion against the revelation of God recorded in the Bible. Scripture has lifted the veil of confusion about the nature of God and what he has declared about the questions we perceive to comprise a worldview.

These data from personal interviews with expert teachers agree with the literature on the direct connection between worldview formation and working through values, ethics, and moral dilemmas—both individually and interpersonally. The latter has special importance because it equips students with abilities to discern and interact respectfully with each other's perspectives, thus demonstrating the worldview concept as a lived reality of intersecting narratives rife with the potential for conflict.

The interview data contain some hints toward moving away from the transmissional model of pedagogy that relies heavily on cognitive and theoretical instruction comprised of lectures, individual assignments, and research papers. However, these hints appear more in the conversations with the participants than the evidence from the triangulation data. Course syllabi and college catalogs still tend to portray the transmissional model with its focus on quizzes, tests, research papers, and lectures. Notable exceptions include the use of field trips, tactile learning, in-class debates, and stimulating visual teaching aids. The literature supports these as preferred forms of pedagogy for worldview formation. Nevertheless, some surprising inconsistencies with the literature also arose in the data. For example, student readiness for engagement in the concepts and issues was a predominant factor throughout the interviews but was less so in the literature. Participants also spoke much more about the potential for negative influence by the teacher than any of the works in the literature review. In addition, those interviewed made little mention of the co-curricular contributions of college life to worldview formation, apart from informal interactions. Finally, none of the schools represented here have investigated the worldview assessment tools that were discovered in the literature. A survey of these tools that evaluates their strengths and weaknesses should be done and published for the benefit of Bible college faculty.

Overall, two notable metaphors arose from the data. First, the image of throwing a puzzle into the air and then reassembling it together is an excellent portrayal of the deconstruction and reconstruction process. Second, the image of teachers setting a trajectory that guides students forward as lifelong learners who anticipate engaging in complex issues and tough decisions that are rooted in a strong Christian worldview. The following chapter turns to evaluating and interpreting these data resulting in a new model for worldview pedagogy based on logical connectivity with the research data.

5

Discussion and Conclusion

To date, only emerging qualitative data exist on pedagogy employed specifically for worldview formation, especially in Christian contexts. In keeping with the aim of grounded theory, I carried out this qualitative research using personal interviews for the goal of discovering a theory for the processes expert teachers use in employing effective worldview pedagogy. This stage of the research involves a discussion of the findings and presentation of a theoretical model grounded in the data. Birks and Mills describe such a model as "an explanatory scheme comprising a set of concepts related to each other through logical patterns of connectivity" (2015, p. 108).

To accomplish the purpose of this study, I explored the following questions that align with the selected problem and intent of the research:

1. What instructional designs and pedagogical methods are especially effective for raising worldview awareness and shaping Christian worldview development?
2. How does the worldview of the teacher and his or her relationships with students influence pedagogical effectiveness?
3. How are teachers assessing college students for worldview awareness and development?

DISCUSSION AND CONCLUSION

Question One: Instructional Design and Pedagogical Methods

This study demonstrates validity through findings that are comparable to several areas in the established literature—namely, in matters of learning objectives, cultural engagement, the inadequacies of strict transmissional approaches, and the value of active learning strategies. However, this research also brings legitimate additions to the literature through a reliable methodology yielding credible data. The following sections are presented as worthy of attention for Bible college educators.

Preliminary knowledge to consider

A sound instructional design and pedagogical methodology for Christian worldview formation must begin with clarifying a few significant preliminary factors. Chief among these would be the personal presuppositions toward the worldview concept. There were four stances observed among the interview participants: a) indifference, b) rejection, c) caution, and d) enthusiasm. However, regardless of a professor's standpoint, the implicit nature of worldview development occurs in students throughout the college experience.

Perhaps what is more important to a teacher than attitude or terminology is clarifying what they are contending for as an educator. The data in this research reveal different yet complementary aspects of formation that find their way into worldview pedagogy. For example, one participant held a strong passion for asserting the existence of absolute truth. Another repeatedly expressed a hunger to convince his students to place their lives in the unfolding story of God's purposes in this world. A history professor interviewed for this research openly claims he does not primarily want his students to come away with a love of history. Rather, he wants them to develop critical thinking and greater relevance for contemporary living through learning skills in hermeneutics and empathy. Overall, a teacher's passion will certainly come through, but it will be just one component that contributes to a student's worldview formation.

Teachers in Bible colleges are constrained by the levels of personal maturity and cognitive development students bring to the institution. In addition, as Kanitz (2005) points out, there are several variations of Christian worldview stemming from diverse interpretive communities. These also set limits on a student's overall readiness to move forward in worldview formation. Therefore, a college educational experience is just one of several influences upon a student's worldview. As Kanitz puts it, "we are not starting with open plots ready for cultivation; we are starting with densely populated intellectual ground with various worldviews firmly entrenched and others competing for space. This presents enormous pedagogical challenges" (2005, p. 105). A teacher's posture towards control or conformity here makes a vital difference in student receptivity.

Acree's (2003) advice to assume a piecemeal approach as the norm in today's students is noteworthy at this stage. She refers to student ignorance or dualism concerning contradictions between biblical values and secular theories. The situation is curious and concerning. For example, I have experienced several encounters with undergraduate students who expressed reticence to theological perspectives being included in behavioral and social science-based general studies courses. Wolf's (2011) warnings about naturalism explain the cause for concern. Students are attracted to the methodology and knowledge base that exists in the behavioral and social sciences, but do struggle to resolve the worldview principles by which these disciplines explain human behavior and social phenomena as strictly part of the natural, empirical world. The situation reflects Wilson's (2000; 1998) prediction that the study of ethics would be taken out of the hands of philosophers and *biologized*. The term means to assimilate a subject into a biological framework or context, and hence, a naturalistic worldview, which was a burgeoning perspective at the time of Wilson's original writing. Haidt (2012) also alludes to Wilson's prediction in suggesting that a person's right or left-leaning values concerning religion or politics might be rooted in their genetic makeup.

In short, the situation centers on the concern that students often end up bifurcating the metaphysical and epistemological understandings rather than integrating them. Typically, this is because they fear the integration will be done poorly, thus leaving the social science knowledge base seriously diluted. As a result, I recommend that faculty anticipate ignorance or inconsistencies in a student's presuppositions, then plan content and pedagogical practices that push students to wrestle with theological reflection.

Nevertheless, I affirm the benefits of learning from a knowledge base that represents a non-Christian worldview. Ironically, there are even biblical examples of learning from those outside the community of God's people. Some examples include the proverbs from Agur and King Lemuel (Pr. 30:1—31:31) and the thirty sayings from the wise in Proverbs 22:17—24:22, which are generally accepted by scholars as influenced by the Teaching of Amenemope—an ancient Egyptian wisdom text. Goldingay says this reflects "the theological conviction that the God of Israel is God of all nations and of all of life. It is not therefore surprising when other peoples perceive truths about life which the people of God can also profit from" (1994, p. 602). Therefore, I suggest the tension with Christian worldview and naturalism could be mitigated for believers through two realizations: a) that people usually do not exemplify any single worldview in pure form; our real lives are a composite of multiple influences even if we hold to a dominant confessional belief system (Wilkens & Sanford, 2009), and b) appreciation for the insights gained through naturalism can be viewed as common ground between believers and non-believers when viewed as mutually profitable knowledge (i.e., general revelation) which lies outside the scope of God's special revelation (Pinnock, 2000)

Tools to employ during instructional design

From the outset, a faculty member must keep a variety of educational philosophies in mind as they draft learning objectives. A Protestant evangelical approach to education tends to be expressed through a tradition rooted in Theistic Realism, Essentialist, and Behaviorist assumptions. However, the personal interviews and triangulation data from this research reveal many learning objectives that would be better served through an educational philosophy informed by cognitive-constructivism and humanist characteristics. Adopting a design based on these philosophies in certain courses can equip students for the leadership development and critical thinking skills needed for serving society and the Church. For example, a constructivist pedagogy—learner-centered, inquiry guided, and problem-based—can feature more active learning, customizable assignments, and engagement with issues relevant to student roles as pastors and Christian leaders.

Institutional life has a way of pushing philosophical reflection off the daily schedule, especially for busy administrative faculty. However, an instructional design with learning outcomes aimed at deepening students' knowledge, equipping them for group decision-making, or providing introspective, experiential learning that is delivered primarily through lectures and a set of objective tests is a mismatched experience for students. The design should fit the objectives of instruction. This was an area of concern observed in certain syllabi submitted as triangulation data. This is an area where deans or expert faculty can step in to assist professors struggling with lackluster instructional design. Effective teachers know how to design learning environments where methods match objectives. This makes holistic learning possible (Merrill et al., 1996). Student satisfaction is an important focus of assessment and a well-planned, engaging instructional design is an area where this is felt strongly.

Finally, in reflecting on the concerns from the participants about student readiness, I recommend that Christian institutions begin to gather and share data from survey instruments such as the College Student Inventory™ from Ruffalo Noel-Levitz, which help faculty identify leading non-cognitive indicators of students' success, retention, and persistence. Such information would help teachers differentiate instruction to suit specific readiness challenges.

Pedagogical methods in the classroom

Knowledge is valuable, but knowledge alone cannot persuade a student to learn. A teacher's influence must touch the emotions as well, so it is essential for the teacher to show genuine enthusiasm for the topic. Shamp-Ellis and Cross (2009) lament how often messages about effective pedagogy are presented solely as gaining skills in classroom management, sensitivity to situational awareness, or the application of a variety of teaching strategies. Conversely, they posit a more important question: how do teachers personally relate to the subject matter? Their hope is that educators understand that a teacher's immediacy—what they call *being there*—through a sincere "display of enthusiasm or passion for the topic itself, the learners, and the involvement of the topic with self, students, and the world is rewarding to both the teacher and the students" (Shamp-Ellis & Cross, 2009, para. 14).

Teachers in Christian environments must let this aspect of themselves show if they are to be the "salty lights" (cf. Matthew 5:13-14) described by Shamp-Ellis and Cross. For instance, a faculty member once told me that students likely respond well to his teaching because he shows a contagious passion in the classroom. Such pedagogy is a testimony of a teacher's own joy and wonder in being formed into a reflection of Christ. In fact, throughout the interviews for this research the participants would get excited when they talked about their subject matter, especially in the context of what they are contending for in student worldview formation.

The literature review and personal interviews in this research serve to confirm the tremendous value of incorporating active learning. While this approach should not be overstated, given that a variety of teaching approaches is more effective than a single method (Hetzel & Walters, 2007), my observations of the triangulation data suggest its use is marginal in some of the participants' courses. Academic deans can use faculty development sessions to review excellent articles such as Jordan, Bawden, and Bergmann (2008) or Collier and Dowson (2008), which expose faculty to methods other than the transmissional educational model, which could be described as McDonaldized (Ritzer, 2011)—i.e., marked by mundane routine, irrational standards, and homogenized culture. Incorporating more of the student-centered and active learning seen in the transformational model (Collier & Dowson, 2008) would serve the purposes of worldview pedagogy well.

Question Two: The Teacher's Worldview and Relationship with Students

This area shapes the posture of the relationship between teachers and students. Certainly, every teacher sets an example, but what constitutes a good example from the faculty toward students in Christian higher education? Hetzel and Walters' (2007) research confirms the top value that students hold toward faculty is that they demonstrate Christian ethics in interactions with others as well as an ability to integrate Christian worldview into their course content.

Participants in this research emphasized that equipping students for relevance and conscious empathy is a critical aspect of pedagogy for Christian worldview formation. The skill is sometimes referred to as cultural competence, which I adapted from Segen ("Cultural Competence," 2006) and define as the ability to appreciate what is commendable, articulate what is compatible and incompatible, and interact respectfully with persons from cultures and/or belief systems other than one's own, based on a range of factors. This ability relies heavily on a person's metacognition—i.e., awareness and understanding of their own thought processes. The literature as well as this research confirm that students often learn this ability from their teacher. These data remind teachers to be more thoughtful about their communication style, especially in the classroom. It is tempting for a teacher, in the pursuit of classroom vivacity, to end up portraying themselves poorly. For example, humor, sarcasm, and teasing do not always connect with students, especially those from differing cultures and church traditions. Overall, a teacher's passion for the topic and its relation to Christian worldview, coupled with a mature posture toward social consciousness, sets a favorable context for student formation.

Question Three: Assessing Worldview Awareness and Development

All schools represented in this research are struggling to assess how students acquire and express a biblical worldview. However, the insight of assessing by small gains is a helpful approach given that Bible colleges cannot produce in students a fully developed worldview through a single course or academic program and then measure it on a simple test. A worldview continues to form long after a student leaves college. Moreover, Peabody offers a helpful insight in his Christmas-themed article, saying, "in reflecting on the birth of Christ, here's what I realized: Jesus becoming a baby automatically put God's seal of approval on a slow process . . . Grace for slowness is built into the very nature of the Incarnation." (2015, para. 6, 10).

This perspective raises a question of the value of assessment tools that reduce the indicators of a Christian worldview to a succinct group of multiple choice answers that are testing for propositional conformity. Such things could be taught in a first-year doctrinal survey course. The approach seems so antithetical to what the interview participants hope to see as growth in their students.

There are some professors who prefer objective formats that rely on quantitative data for assessment, while others prefer more subjective approaches that rely on a student demonstrating application of knowledge for assessment, despite being more labor intensive. Overall, if the college can gather assessment data from multiple sources, each of which demonstrate student achievement on specific components of worldview, then a valid and reliable form of assessment is possible.

For example, I would argue the foremost components of the secular western worldview today are scientific naturalism (what is prime reality and truth), humanism (who is of prime importance), individualism (one's identity in society), progressivism (what is best for improving society and the human condition), consumerism (marks of success; purpose of stewardship), and an ethical system rooted in situationism (do whatever is deemed loving), consequentialist principles (do whatever you want as long as it does not hurt others) and sensualism (feelings are the primary criterion for what is good and gives direction to cognition). Each of these areas can be addressed and assessed in college courses on ethics, biblical theology, psychology, and even administration. Therefore, it is conceivable to observe students' growth over time in testing and approving God's will in these matters (cf. Romans 12:2) as they seek to understand what it is to be a people set apart for God in contrast to the worldviews around them.

Proposed Model for Worldview Pedagogy in Bible Colleges

The themes discovered in this research provide the elements of a plausible model for guiding pedagogy for Christian worldview formation. The model shown in Figure 1 incorporates these four themes:

Clarity on goal

This involves the preliminary factors influencing the teacher, the curriculum, and the students. First, a teacher should have clarity on what aspect of Christian worldview formation they are attempting to affect. Because there are several components to a worldview that a college education can address, teachers should focus their efforts on what they are equipped to do well within their scope of the curriculum. No single teacher or course will cover all aspects of worldview development. The limitations that come into play here include the overall length of time for a student's chosen college program, which can be from one to four years or more. In addition, the cognitive abilities of students are a potential limitation because these vary in the typical 18 to 22-year-old undergraduate population. Some legitimate dangers exist here as well, mostly in the form of the teacher's posture toward worldview education, which could involve excessive control over outcomes or displaying a lack of sensitivity toward various expressions of Christian worldview represented in the student body and larger church community.

Relevant holistic objectives

The attention here is on creating a sound instructional design that brings greater coherence between the world the student experiences and the Christian values that apply to it. In addition, the learning should be paced to match the gradual development of a worldview typical to human experience. This might challenge the amount of coverage curriculum designers would like to accomplish in a program, but a more reasonable pace will have a better effect on students. Some specific dangers at this point would be designing learning objectives that focus on propositional content for recitation apart from a measure of personal transformation. However, even a set of relevant and engaging learning objectives cannot motivate students that are too distracted by elements of popular culture and do not apply the critical engagement necessary to recognize and reshape their presuppositions.

D-R continuum + active learning

This portion of the model represents the most common pedagogical methods used by the participants. The D-R continuum means using a scope of pedagogy that moves along a continuum of deconstruction and reconstruction strategies for testing and remaking the perspectives students bring to the topic at hand. Using this in combination with a variety of active learning approaches, especially where the teacher participates with the students, sets the posture for the learning relationships. When students experience the metaphorical "throwing the puzzle in the air," they must have supportive relationships with fellow students and the teacher to make the D-R continuum experience constructive.

The limitations within this theme are set by students' critical thinking skills and life experiences. This affects their ability to process their beliefs system and the liminal moments when transformation is possible. In addition, the extent of their life experience gives them resources to draw upon for reflection and application. A crucial limitation can exist for certain students that struggle with psychological injuries because worldviews are deeply affected by traumatic events, which can alter a person's unconscious assumptions (Kennedy & Humphreys, 1994). The foremost danger during this aspect of worldview pedagogy is spending too much time on deconstruction to the point where students are left with more questions than useful answers or even irritated by an instructional approach that just criticizes rather than constructs beliefs systems.

This aspect of the model also creates liminal moments in the learning experience, which means students are put into a transitional or initial stage of the process. Interestingly, liminality is something all Christians experience as part of their worldview due to the theological concept known as "already, but not yet," which is an interpretation of the kingdom of God known as inaugurated eschatology. The idea is attributed to Ladd (1959) who concluded the kingdom of God is both present and future reality. Thus, liminality is experienced as a type of threshold where Christians no longer hold their previous worldview but have not fully realized the eternal worldview that awaits them when the consummation is complete.

Assessment data

Data compiled from multiple assessment tools, each looking at a different aspect of formation, will demonstrate whether the institution is accomplishing its learning objectives related to forming a biblical worldview in students. These data can in turn be used to improve knowledge of the preliminary factors, the health of learning relationships, and the effectiveness of the instructional design. Assessment tools should focus on specific components of worldview development related to the learning objectives, then measure small gains in keeping with an appropriate pace of formation. Ideally, instruction and assessment should include propositional areas as well as behavioral and heart-orientations. Of course, beneficial assessment depends on a key limiting factor—namely, the amount of time the student stays in college.

SETTING A SUSTAINABLE TRAJECTORY

1. Clarity on goal

Identify the preliminary factors within students, teachers, and the curriculum.

Limitations: length of college program; individual cognitive abilities; primary or secondary emphasis on worldview in the curriculum.

Dangers: too broad of a focus; the teacher's negative posture, excessive control, and lack of sensitivity.

2. Relevant holistic outcomes

Instructional design that brings greater coherence.

Limitations: an appropriate amount of coverage paced for a slow process.

Dangers: strictly propositional focus; students are too distracted and unprepared for critical engagement.

3. D-R continuum + active learning

Pedagogical methods that set the posture of learning relationships.

Limitations: students' critical thinking skills and life experiences.

Dangers: creating more questions than useful answers.

4. Assess specific components

Assessment tools that focus on specific components of worldview development.

Multiple tools that confirm small gains in various component areas; using data to inform improvements to goals, outcomes, and pedagogical methods.

Limitations: students' overall time spent in college.

Dangers: oversimplified assessment.

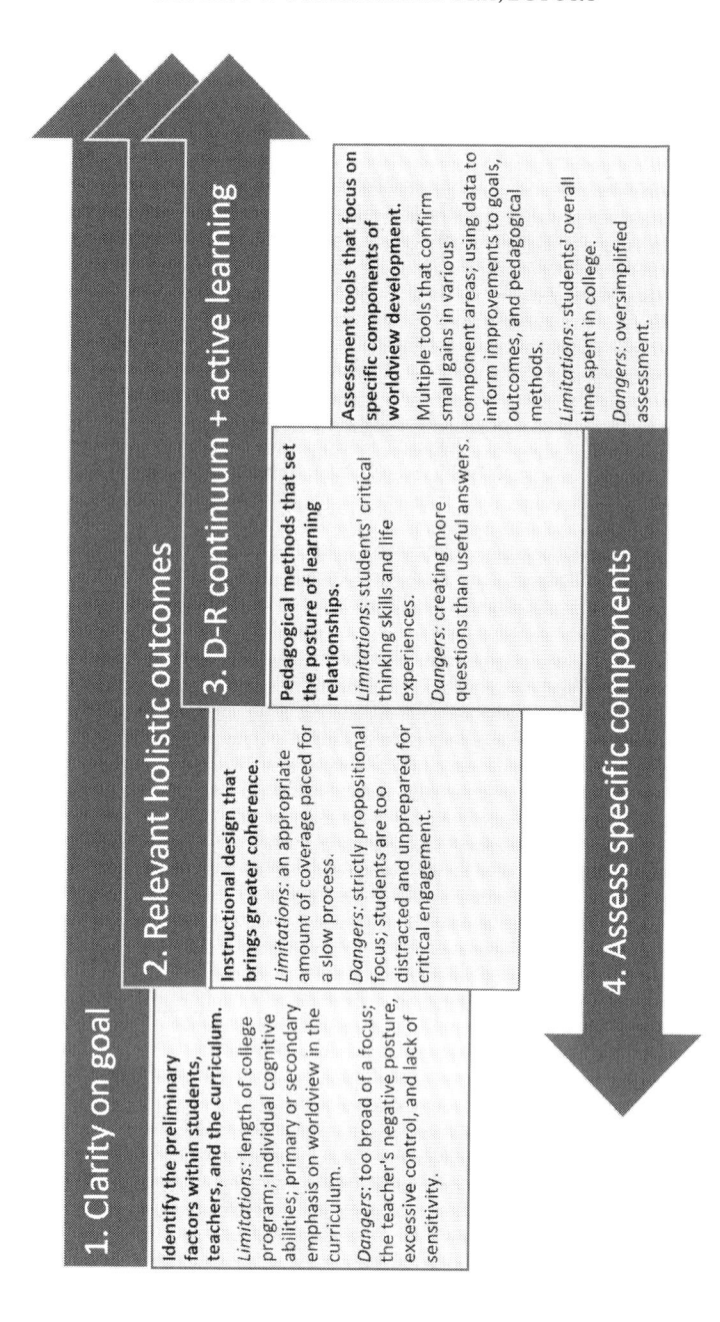

Figure 1: A model for Christian worldview pedagogy.

The four pedagogical goals are represented as an increasing arrow process featuring sequential and overlapping elements. In sum, effective worldview pedagogy should identify vital preliminary factors to help determine a clear goal, use appropriately paced instructional design to achieve relevant and holistic learning outcomes, and pedagogical methods that set an engaging posture for the learning relationships though the use of deconstructing and reconstructing belief systems along with participatory active learning strategies. The model concludes with an assessment approach that measures small gains in the component areas of worldview.

Conclusion

This research should encourage college faculty to speak with clarity and passion on the specific goals they are aiming for in terms of worldview formation, while keeping in mind that no single instructor or course will discuss all aspects of worldview formation. Therefore, faculty members should neither spread their focus too thin nor exercise too much power over the outcome of their pedagogy. In sum, a Christian educator must accept a place of influence, rather than control, over their students' worldview because this formation will continue long after students leave the college environment. For this reason, teachers can resolve to set a sustainable trajectory that the Holy Spirit will continue to direct for years to come.

Assessing various component areas of a Christian worldview (i.e., propositional, ethical, behavioral, social, and heart-orientations) separately through coordinated tools would be better than attempting to use a single tool that risks oversimplification. Compiling the component pieces of assessment together will gain a superior picture of worldview development over the duration of a college program that builds up students one small gain at a time.

Recommendations for Further Study

Further qualitative work should be done to explore the affective responses of faculty to the worldview concept. Administrators should not assume every faculty member buys into the discussion and sees its inherent value. Moreover, this research revealed some helpful diversity to the worldview concept that allows a mature view to guide curriculum design forward. Using a broader unit of analysis and greater diversity of participants would strengthen the data and increase the generalizability of the findings. For example, all participants in this study were Caucasian males with strong upbringings in western culture. This certainly gives a limited view of a teacher's approach to this type of formation. Expanding this study to include women and people of various ethnicities would provide more comprehensive data on worldview pedagogy. Ideally, further research would also take the students' perspectives on effective pedagogical methods into consideration, given the fact that they are receiving the pedagogy and experiencing the formation of worldview in the Bible college environment.

The challenges of assessing worldview would be helped by a published review of current assessment tools, explaining both their areas of strengths and limitations. Each assessment tool discovered in this research tends to reflect the worldview and educational philosophy of its creator/designer. In other words, many are propositional in nature, which indicates an essentialist educational approach to instruction and assessment. Others appear more constructivist in approach, emphasizing theological integration, problem-solving, and group processes.

Finally, further research could consider how an institution might assess ongoing worldview development in their alumni. For example, Fox (2007) takes a similar route by investigating the relationship between alumni satisfaction with their Bible college education and their persistence in ministry. Also, Cardwell and Hunt's (1979) longitudinal study with over one thousand seminary students reports on the relationship between persistence and the type of training received from seminary. These examples raise the question on the relationship between student satisfaction with their Bible college education and the trajectory of their continuing worldview development.

Improving Christian worldview pedagogy is an important research topic for the college environment. For many students, these are crucial years where faith and learning become personalized through a process of slow but steady worldview transformation. This research offers important insights into not only what educators teach concerning worldview, but how they teach it effectively. This study shows that both are major influences on worldview formation.

Appendix A

Interview Guide Questions

Background information:

1. How do you feel about the concept of worldview and how did you become educated on it?
2. How does worldview formation influence the objectives of your teaching ministry?

Pedagogical practice:

3. What things do you do in your instructional design and pedagogical methods to raise worldview awareness in students?
4. What is your pedagogical goal for Christian worldview formation?
5. How does your own worldview and your relationships with students influence their development of a Christian worldview? How do these enhance your teaching effectiveness? Are there any cautions you would recommend?
6. What ways are you assessing college students for worldview awareness and development?

Appendix B

Email Request for Letter of Cooperation —President or Dean

My name is Rob Lindemann and I am a doctoral student at George Fox University in Newberg, Oregon. As part of completing my Ed.D, I am conducting grounded theory research into pedagogical practices for Christian worldview formation. In sum, I am seeking your cooperation by identifying faculty who, in your estimation, are particularly effective at forming Christian worldview in college students.

More specifically, I am inviting you to nominate a faculty member from your institution to participate in about an hour-long personal interview regarding their approaches to teaching that either directly or indirectly aims to form the worldview of college students. The questions will be about their background knowledge of Christian worldview, the factors they take into account when preparing material, their teaching methods, and the assessment strategies they employ. In addition, I will request to examine some institutional materials such as course syllabi, rubrics, and assessment tools or data. The purpose for this is to triangulate the data through two or more methods in order to validate the results.

The objective of this research is to find a theory or model that explains effective teaching for Christian worldview formation. The results of this study will be used for research purposes and may be used for subsequent presentation and/or academic publication.

APPENDIX B: EMAIL REQUEST FOR LETTER OF COOPERATION

Information will be analyzed and presented in a confidential fashion so that no institutional personnel or programs will be identified. I affirm to keep any personal information and identities confidential. All research materials (i.e., audio recordings, transcripts, and signed cooperation forms) will be locked in separate, secure locations for a period of no less than three years. I will be the only individual who will have access to these materials. After three years, I will personally destroy all relevant materials and delete the audio recordings.

I thank you for your time and for considering this project. If you choose to nominate and allow access to triangulation data, please be aware that you are making a contribution to educational research. I would happy to share my findings with you when this project is completed. For your convenience I have attached a template letter of cooperation you can copy onto your institution's letterhead, insert the appropriate details, edit wherever you feel appropriate, and email back to me for my research requirements. If you have any questions regarding this research, please contact me at rlindemann@horizon.edu. If you have any additional questions, you may contact my dissertation chair, Dr. Patrick Allen, at pallen@georgefox.edu or (503) 554-2858.

Appendix C
Letter of Consent—Participant

My name is Rob Lindemann and I am a doctoral student at George Fox University in Newberg, Oregon. As part of completing my Ed.D, I am conducting grounded theory research into pedagogical practices for Christian worldview formation. Your president or academic dean has nominated you as a faculty that is particularly effective at forming Christian worldview in college students.

I am inviting you to engage in about an hour-long personal interview regarding your approaches to teaching that either directly or indirectly aims to form the worldview of college students. The questions will be about your background knowledge of Christian worldview, the factors you take into account when preparing material, your teaching methods, and the assessment strategies you employ. In addition, I will request to examine some institutional materials such as course syllabi, rubrics, and assessment tools or data. The purpose for this is to triangulate the data through two (or more) methods in order to validate the results.

The objective of this research is to find a theory or model that explains effective teaching for Christian worldview formation. The results of this study will be used for research purposes and may be used for subsequent presentation and/or academic publication.

The risks associated with this research are minimal. The personal interview questions are general and should not create any distress. Nevertheless, please be aware that your participation is

APPENDIX C: LETTER OF CONSENT—PARTICIPANT

voluntary and you may decline to continue at any time or decline to answer any question at your discretion. The interview can be conducted via Skype connection and will be audio recorded then later transcribed. Information will be analyzed and presented in a confidential fashion so that no individual will be personally identified. I affirm to keep any personal information and identities confidential.

All research materials (i.e., audio recordings, transcripts, and signed consent forms) will be digitally stored to a secure cloud-based service and separate hard drive – all password protected. I will be the only individual who will have access to these materials. After three years, I will personally destroy all relevant materials and delete the audio recordings.

I thank you for your time and for considering this project. If you choose to participate, please be aware that you are making a contribution to educational research. I would happy to share my findings with you when this project is completed. If you have any questions regarding this research, please contact me at rlindemann@horizon.edu. If you have any additional questions, you may contact my dissertation chair, Dr. Patrick Allen, at pallen@georgefox.edu or (503) 554 – 2858.

If you understand the use of this research and consent to participate, please sign below and send this form back to me.

Participant signature: _____

Researcher signature: _____

Bibliography

Abshier, R. G. (2006). *Classical Christian education: Developing a biblical worldview in the 21st century.* (Master's thesis), Reformed Theological Seminary, Jackson, MI. Retrieved from http://www.tren.com/e-docs/search_w_preview.cfm?p083-0043 Theological Research Exchange Network database.

Acree, A. (2003). *Instilling a biblical worldview by addressing postmodernity: Best practices of postsecondary Christian faculty.* (Unpublished doctoral disseration), Oral Roberts University, Tulsa, OK.

Ahern, K. J. (1999). Ten tips for reflexive bracketing. *Qualitative Health Research, 9*(3), 407-411. doi:10.1177/104973239900900309

Allen, M. J. (2003). *Assessing academic programs in higher education.* San Francisco, CA: Jossey-Bass.

Anderson, B. (1996). Personality and character development: The teacher-learner relationship. *Journal of Christian Education, 39*(1), 17-29.

Anderson, R. C. (1977). The notion of schemata and the educational enterprise: General discussion of the conference. In R. C. Anderson, R. J. Spiro, & W. E. Montague (Eds.), *Schooling and the acquisition of knowledge* (pp. 415-431). Hillsdale, NJ: Lawrence Erlbaum Associates.

Armstrong, D., & McMahon, B. (2000, September). *Transformational pedagogy: Practitioners' perspectives.* Paper presented at the 5th Annual Values and Educational Leadership Conference, Bridgetown, Barbados.

Ausubel, D. P. (1960). The use of advance organizers in the learning and retention of meaningful verbal material. *Journal of Educational Psychology, 51*(5), 267-272.

Badii, R., & Fabbri, E. (2011). Framing our world,or: Reconsidering the idea of Weltbild. *Humana.Mente Journal of Philosophical Studies, 18,* iii-xxix.

Badley, K. (1994). The faith/learning integration movement in Christian higher education: Slogan or substance? *Journal of Research on Christian Education, 3*(1), 13-33. doi:10.1080/10656219409484798

Bain, K. (2004). *What the best college teachers do.* Cambridge, MA: Harvard University Press.

BIBLIOGRAPHY

Barron, W. L. (2010). *An ethical pedagogy for contemporary culture: Educating high school juniors and seniors in a Christian ethical model.* (Doctoral dissertation), Erskine Theological Seminary, Due West, SC. Available from Theological Research Exchange Network database.

Bartolomé, L. (2007). Critical pedagogy and teacher education. In P. McLaren & J. Kincholoe (Eds.), *Critical pedagogy: Where are we now?* (pp. 289-314). New York, NY: Peter Lang.

Bass, B. M. (1985). *Leadership and performance beyond expectations.* New York, NY: Free.

Baumann, E. K. (2011). *Worldview as worship: The dynamics of a transformative Christian education.* Eugene, OR: Wipf & Stock.

Belcher, E. C. (2009). Is the heart of education the education of the heart? *ICCTE Journal, 2*(1).

Belcher, E. C., & Parr, G. (2011). Exploring worldview and identity in an institution of Christian higher education. *Research and Development in Higher Education, 34,* 40-49.

Bertrand, J. M. (2007). *Rethinking worldview: Learning to think, live, and speak in this world.* Wheaton, IL: Crossway.

Birks, M., & Mills, J. (2015). *Grounded theory: A practical guide.* Thousand Oaks, CA: SAGE Publications.

Boise Bible College - Doctrinal Position. (2014). Retrieved from http://www.boisebible.edu/admissions/bbc-doctrinal-position

Bowen, G. A. (2006). Grounded theory and sensitizing concepts. *International Journal of Qualitative Methods, 5*(3), 12-23.

Boyatzis, R. (1998). *Transforming qualitative information: Thematic analysis and code development.* Thousand Oaks, CA: Sage.

Brickhill, C. E. (2010). *A comparative analysis of factors influencing the development of a biblical worldview in Christian middle-school students.* (Doctoral dissertation), Liberty University, Lynchburg, VA. Retrieved from http://digitalcommons.liberty.edu/doctoral/370/

Brooks, A. K. (2000). Transformation. In E. Hayes & D. Flannery (Eds.), *Women as learners: The significance of gender in adult learning.* San Francisco, CA: Jossey-Bass.

Brown, B. (2006). Shame resilience theory: A grounded theory study on women and shame. *Families in Society, 87*(1), 43-52. doi:10.1606/1044-3894.3483

———. (2012). *Daring greatly: How the courage to be vulnerable transforms the way we live, love, parent, and lead.* New York, NY: Gotham.

Bryant, M. H. (2008). *A comparative analysis of factors contributing to the biblical worldview among high school students in the American Association of Christian Schools of Georgia, North Carolina, and South Carolina* (Doctoral dissertation), Liberty University, Lynchburg, VA. Retrieved from http://digitalcommons.liberty.edu/doctoral/1027/

Bufford, R. K. (2007). Philosophical foundations for clinical supervision within a Christian worldview. *Journal of Psychology and Christianity, 26*(4), 293-297.

BIBLIOGRAPHY

Burnett, D. (1990). *Clash of worlds*. Eastbourne, UK: MARC.

Carpenter, D. M. (2015). Worldview, Christian maturity, and young adulthood: The what, when, where, and how of education after high school. In W. Jeynes & E. Martinez (Eds.), *Ministering spiritually to families* (pp. 131-143): Springer International.

Carpenter, D. R. (2007). Phenomenology as method. In H. J. Streubert & D. R. Carpenter (Eds.), *Qualitative research in nursing: Advancing the humanistic imperative*. Philadelphia, PA: Lippincott.

Carr, N., & Mitchell, J. (2007). The neglected role of religion and worldview in schooling for wisdom, character, and virtue. In D. N. Aspin & J. D. Chapman (Eds.), *Values education and lifelong learning* (Vol. 10, pp. 295-314): Springer Netherlands.

Chan, Y.-C., & Wong, N.-Y. (2014). Worldviews, religions, and beliefs about teaching and learning: Perception of mathematics teachers with different religious backgrounds. *Educational Studies in Mathematics, 87*(3), 251-277. doi:10.1007/s10649-014-9555-1

Charmaz, K. (2000). Grounded theory: Objectivist and constructivist methods. In N. Denzin & Y. Lincoln (Eds.), *Handbook of qualitative research* (2nd ed., pp. 509-535). Thousand Oaks, CA: SAGE.

Charmaz, K. (2014). *Constructing grounded theory: A practical guide through qualitative analysis*. Thousand Oaks, CA: SAGE Publications Inc.

Clarke, A. (2005). *Situational analysis: Grounded theory after the postmodern turn*. Thousand Oaks, CA: SAGE Publications.

Cobern, W. (1996). Worldview theory and conceptual change in science education. *Science Education, 80*(5), 579-610.

Cohen, L. M., & Gelbrich, J. (1999). Task 4: What is my philosophy of education? Retrieved from http://oregonstate.edu/instruct/ed416/Task4.html

Collier, J., & Dowson, M. (2008). Beyond transmissional pedagogies in Christian education: One school's recasting of values education. *Journal of Research on Christian Education, 17*(2), 199-216. doi:10.1080/10656210802433418

Continuum. (2011). *Concise Oxford English Dictionary*. Oxford, UK: Oxford University Press.

Cooling, T. (1994). *A Christian vision for state education*. London SPCK.

Creswell, J. W. (2002). *Educational research: Planning, conducting, and evaluating quantitative and qualitative research*. Upper Saddle River, NJ: Pearson Education.

———. (2013). *Qualitative inquiry and research design: Choosing among five approaches* (3rd ed.). Thousand Oaks, CA: SAGE Publications, Inc.

Cultural Competence. (2006). In J. C. Segen (Ed.), *Concise dictionary of modern medicine*. New York, NY: McGraw-Hill

Danaher, W. (2009). Reconstructing Christian ethics: Exploring constructivist practices for teaching Christian ethics in the masters of divinity curriculum. *Teaching Theology and Religion, 12*(2), 101-108.

BIBLIOGRAPHY

Daniels, D., Franz, R., & Wong, K. (2000). A classroom with a worldview: Making spiritual assumptions explicit in management education. *Journal of Management Education, 24*(5), 540-561.

Darko, L. J. (2009). *Student leadership development: A case study.* (Master's thesis). Retrieved from http://research.avondale.edu.au/cgi/viewcontent. cgi?article=1013&context=theses_masters_coursework

de Oliveira, P. C. (2006). *Developing an interdisciplinary analysis and application of worldview concepts for Christian mission.* (Unpublished doctoral dissertation), Andrews University, Seventh Day Adventist Theological Seminary, Berrien Springs, MI.

Deckard, S. (1998). *Creation Worldview Test (Version CWT-01).* Lexington, KY: Nehemiah Institute, Inc.

Dilthey, W. (1989). *Wilhelm Dilthey: Selected works, Vol. 1: Introduction to the human sciences* (R. A. Makkreel & F. Rodi Eds. Vol. 1). Princeton, NJ: Princeton University Press.

Dolan, R. P. (2010). *Christian students' worldviews and propensity for mission teaching.* (Doctoral dissertation), Liberty University, Lynchburg, VA. Retrieved from http://digitalcommons.liberty.edu/doctoral/410/

Dunaway, J. M. (2005). *Gladly learn, gladly teach: Living out one's calling in the twenty-first century academy.* Macon, GA Mercer University Press

Edlin, R. (2009). Christian education and worldview. *ICCTE Journal, 3*(2).

Estep, J. R., Anthony, M. J., & Allison, G. R. (2008). *A theology for Christian education.* Nashville, TN: B & H Publishing Group.

Expert. (2003). In F. C. Mish (Ed.), *Merriam-Webster's Collegiate Dictionary.* Springfield, MA: Merriam-Webster, Inc.

Fong, M. (2009). The spirit moves where there is a need in higher education. *Directions for Teaching and Learning, 120*(Winter 2009), 87-95. doi:DOI: 10.1002/tl.380

Fowler, S., Dickens, K., & Beech, G. (n.d.). *Body of knowledge.* Retrieved from Mulgoa, NSW, Australia http://www.nice.edu.au/resources/NICE_body_ of_knowledge.pdf

Fox, D. (2007). Preparing for ministry in a Bible college. *Biblical Higher Education Journal*(Winter), 51-63.

Fyock, J. A. (2008). *The effect of teacher's worldviews on the worldviews of high school seniors.* (Doctoral dissertation), Liberty University, Lynchburg, VA. Retrieved from http://digitalcommons.liberty.edu/cgi/viewcontent.cgi?ar ticle=1113&context=doctoral

Galindo, I. (1998). *The craft of Christian teaching: Essentials for becoming a very good teacher.* Cambridge, MS: Judson.

Geisler, N. L., & Watkins, W. D. (1989). *Worlds apart: A handbook on world views* (2nd ed.). Grand Rapids, MI: Baker.

Glanzer, P., & Talbert, T. (2005). The impact and implications of faith or worldviews in the classroom. *Journal of Research in Character Education, 3*(1), 25-42.

BIBLIOGRAPHY

Glaser, B. (1998). *Doing grounded theory: Issues and discussion.* Mill Valley, CA: Sociology.

Glaser, B., & Strauss, A. L. (1967). *The discovery of grounded theory: Strategies for qualitative research.* New York, NY: Aldine.

Goldingay, J. (1994). Proverbs. In D. A. Carson (Ed.), *New Bible commentary: 21st century edition.* Downers Grove, Ill: Inter-Varsity.

Grace Bible College - President's Letter. (2013). Retrieved from http://www.gbcol.edu/about-grace/president-s-letter

Grauf-Grounds, C., Edwards, S., Macdonald, D., Mui-Teng Quek, K., & Schermer Sellers, T. (2009). Developing graduate curricula faithful to professional training and Christian worldview. *Christian Higher Education, 8*(1), 1-17. doi:10.1080/15363750802134931

Haidt, J. (2012). *The righteous mind: Why good people are divided by politics and religion.* New York, NY: Pantheon.

Harris, R. A. (2004). *The integration of faith and learning: A worldview approach.* Eugene, OR: Wipf and Stock.

Hattie, J. A. (2003). Teachers make a difference: What is the research evidence? Paper presented at the Australian Council for Educational Research Annual Conference, Melbourne, Austrailia.

Hattie, J. A., & Jaeger, R. J. (2003). Distinguishing expert teachers from experienced and novice teachers: University of Auckland: Australian Council for Educational Research.

Heath, H., & Cowley, S. (2004). Developing a grounded theory approach: A comparison of Glaser and Strauss. *International Journal of Nursing Studies, 41*(2), 141-150. doi:http://dx.doi.org/10.1016/S0020-7489(03)00113-5

Hetzel, J., & Walters, K. (2007). Undergraduates' perceptions of ideal learning environments. *Journal of the International Community of Christians in Teacher Education, 2*(2).

Hiebert, A. (2005). *Character with competence education: The Bible college movement in Canada.* Steinbach, MB: Association of Canadian Bible Colleges.

Hiebert, P. (2008). *Transforming worldviews: An anthropological understanding of how people change.* Grand Rapids, MI: Baker Academic.

Hood, J. C. (2010). Orthodoxy vs. power: The defining traits of grounded theory. In A. Bryant & K. Charmaz (Eds.), *The SAGE handbook of grounded theory* (pp. 151-164). Thousand Oaks, CA: SAGE.

House, R. J., Hanges, P. J., Javidan, M., Dorfman, P. W., & Gupta, V. (2004). *Culture, leadership, and organizations: The GLOBE study of 62 societies.* Thousand Oaks, CA: Sage.

Howell, B. M., & Paris, J. W. (2011). *Introducing cultural anthropology: A Christian perspective.* Grand Rapids, MI: Baker Academic.

Howse, B. S. (n.d). *Worldview Weekend.* Retrieved from www.worldviewweekend.com

BIBLIOGRAPHY

Huitt, W. (1999). Conation as an important factor of mind. *Educational Psychology Interactive*. Retrieved from http://www.edpsycinteractive.org/topics/conation/conation.html

Jacobsen, D., & Jacobsen, R. (2004). *Scholarship and Christian faith: Enlarging the conversation*. New York, NY: Oxford University Press, Inc.

Jordan, N., Bawden, R., & Bergmann, L. (2008). Pedagogy for addressing the worldview challenge in sustainable development of agriculture. *Journal of Natural Resources and Life Sciences Education, 37*.

Kanitz, L. (2005). Improving Christian worldview pedagogy: Going beyond mere Christianity. *Christian Higher Education, 4*(2), 99-108. doi:10.1080/15363750590923101

Kennedy, M., & Humphreys, K. (1994). Understanding worldview transformation in members of mutual help groups. *Prevention in Human Services, 11*(1), 181-191. doi:10.1080/10852359409511202

Knight, G. (2006). *Philosophy and education: An introduction in Christian perspective*. Berrien Springs, MI: Andrews University Press, 4th edition

Koltko-Rivera, M. E. (2004). The psychology of worldviews. *Review of General Psychology, 8*(1), 3-58. doi:10.1037/1089-2680.8.1.3

Krakowski, M. (2008). *Isolation and integration: Education and worldview formation in ultra-orthodox Jewish schools*. (Doctoral dissertation), Northwestern University, Evanston, ILL. ProQuest Dissertations and Theses (UMI No. 3303612) database.

Kurtz, P. (1994). *Living without religion*. Amherst, New York: Prometheus.

Ladd, G. E. (1959). *The gospel of the kingdom: Scriptural studies in the kingdom of God*. Grand Rapids, MI: Eerdmans.

Lee, H. E. (Ed.) (2010). *Faith-based education that constructs*. Eugene, OR: Wipf & Stock.

Lieberman, B. (2012). Brené Brown is a grounded researcher. Retrieved from http://www.dumbofeather.com/conversation/brene-brown-is-a-grounded-researcher/

Lindemann, R. (2008). Constructive politics for Christian organizations. *Biblical Higher Education Journal, 3*(Winter), 59-72.

Makkreel, R. (Summer 2012 Edition). Wilhelm Dilthey. In E. N. Zalta (Ed.), *The Stanford Encyclopedia of Philosophy*

Martin, V. B., & Gynnild, A. (2011). *Grounded theory: The philosophy, method, and work of Barney Glaser*. Boca Raton, FL: BrownWalker.

Masters, G. (2003). Using research to advance professional practice. Paper presented at the Building Teacher Quality (Conference Proceedings).

Matthews, M. (2009a). Science, worldviews and education: An introduction. *Science, Worldviews and Education*, 1-26.

———. (2009b). Teaching the philosophical and worldview components of science. *Science, Worldviews and Education*, 49-80. doi:10.1007/s11191-007-9132-4

Merrill, M. D., Drake, L., Lacy, M. J., & Pratt, J. (1996). Reclaiming instructional design. *Educational Technology, 36*(5), 5-7.

BIBLIOGRAPHY

Meyer, M., & Booker, J. (2001). *Eliciting and analyzing expert judgment: A practical guide* (Vol. 7). Philadelphia, PA: Society for Industrial and Applied Mathematics.

Meyer, R. (2003). *A comparative analysis of the factors contributing to the biblical worldview of students enrolled in a Christian school.* (Unpublished doctoral dissertation), The Southern Baptist Theological Seminary, Nashville, TN.

Mills, J., Bonner, A., & Francis, K. (2006). The development of constructivist grounded theory. *International Journal of Qualitative Methods, 5*(1), Article 3.

Mittwede, S. K. (2013). Cognitive educational approaches as means of envisioning and effecting worldview transformation via theological education. *Journal of Education & Christian Belief, 17*(2), 301-324.

Morales, K. (2013). *An instrument validation for a three-dimensional worldview survey among undergraduate Christian university students using principal components analysis.* (Doctoral dissertation), Liberty University. Retrieved from http://digitalcommons.liberty.edu/doctoral/733

Morse, J. M. (2009). Tussles, tensions, and resolutions. In J. M. Morse, P. Noerager Stern, J. Corbin, B. Bowers, K. Charmaz, & B. Clark (Eds.), *Developing grounded theory: The second generation* (pp. 13-23). Walnut Creek, CA: Left Coast.

Nash, R. H. (1992). *Worldviews in conflict: Choosing Christianity in a world of ideas.* Grand Rapids, MI: Zondervan.

———. (2003). The Myth of a Value-Free Education. Retrieved from http://www.acton.org/pub/religion-liberty/volume-1-number-4/myth-value-free-education

Naugle, D. M. (2002). *Worldview: The history of a concept.* Grand Rapids, MI: Eerdmans.

———. (2004). *Renewing integrity: A Christian worldview and educational practice.* Paper presented at the National Faculty Leadership Conference, Washington, D.C.

Nehemiah Institute. (2006). *PEERS-II Test: Christianity and culture assessment.* Lexington, KY: Nehemiah Institute, Inc.

Nehemiah Institute. (2012). *PEERS Testing.* Retrieved from http://www.nehemiahinstitute.com/peers.php

Noddings, N. (2013). *Caring: A feminine approach to ethics and moral education.* Berkeley, CA: University of California Press.

Peabody, J. (2015). How Christmas confronts my faulty thinking. *Leadership Journal, December 2015.*

Pinnock, C. H. (2000). Revelation. In S. B. Ferguson & J. I. Packer (Eds.), *New dictionary of theology* (pp. 586). Downers Grove, IL: InterVarsity.

Poe, H. L. (2004). *Christianity in the academy.* Grand Rapids, MI: Baker Academy.

Poggenpoel, M., & Myburgh, C. P. H. (2005). Obstacles in qualitative research: Possible solutions. *Educational Administration Quarterly, 26*(2), 304-311.

BIBLIOGRAPHY

Reactive. (2011). *Concise Oxford English Dictionary.* Oxford, UK: Oxford University Press.

Ritzer, G. (2011). *The McDonaldization of society* (6 ed.). Thousand Oaks, CA: Pine Forge.

Rubin, H. J., & Rubin, I. S. (2011). *Qualitative interviewing: The art of hearing data* (3rd ed.). Thousand Oaks, CA: SAGE Publications Ltd.

Ryan, G. W., & Bernard, H. R. (2003). Techniques to identify themes. *Field Methods, 15*(1), 85-109. doi:10.1177/1525822x02239569

Schlitz, M., Vieten, C., & Amorok, T. (2007). *Living deeply: The art and science of transformation in everyday life.* Oakland, CA: New Harbinger Publications.

Schlitz, M., Vieten, C., & Erickson-Freeman, K. (2011). Conscious aging and worldview transformation. *The Journal of Transpersonal Psychology, 43*(2), 223-238.

Schlitz, M., Vieten, C., & Miller, E. M. (2010). Worldview transformation and the development of social consciousness. *Journal of Consciousness Studies, 17*(7-8), 18-36.

Schlitz, M., Vieten, C., Miller, E. M., Homer, K., Peterson, K., & Erickson-Freeman, K. (2011). The worldview literacy project: Exploring new capacities for the 21st century student. *New Horizons for Learning Journal, 9*(1).

Schultz, K. G. (2013). *Developing an instrument for assessing student biblical worldview in Christian K-12 education.* (Doctoral dissertation). Available from ProQuest Dissertations and Theses (UMI No. 3534997)

Schultz, K. G., & Swezey, J. A. (2013). A three-dimensional concept of worldview. *Journal of Research on Christian Education, 22*(3), 227-243. doi:10.1080/10656219.2013.850612

Schutte, K. J. (2008). Fostering an integrated life of purpose in Christian higher education. *Christian Higher Education, 7*(5), 414-433.

Setran, D. P., & Kiesling, C. A. (2013). *Spiritual formation in emerging adulthood: A practical theology for college and young adult ministry.* Grand Rapids, MI: Baker.

Setran, D. P., Wilhoit, J. C., Ratcliff, D., Haase, D. T., & Rozema, L. (2010). Spiritual formation goes to college: Class-related "soul projects" in Christian higher education. *Christian Education Journal, Series 3, 7*(2), 401-422.

Shamp-Ellis, V., & Cross, N. P. (2009). Recalling subject centered enthusiasm: The essence of great teaching. *ICCTE Journal, 4*(2).

Sherr, M., Huff, G., & Curran, M. (2007). Student perceptions of salient indicators of integration of faith and learning (IFL): The Christian vocation model. *Journal of Research on Christian Education, 16*(1), 15-33. doi:10.1080/10656210701381080

Shimabukuro, G. (2008). Toward a pedagogy grounded in Christian spirituality. *Catholic Education: A Journal of Inquiry & Practice, 11*(4), 505-521.

BIBLIOGRAPHY

Sire, J. W. (2004). *Naming the elephant: Worldview as a concept.* Downer's Grove, Ill: InterVarsity.

———. (2009). *The universe next door: A basic worldview catalog* (4th ed.). Downer's Grove, Ill: InterVarsity.

Smith, C. (2009). *Souls in transition: The religious and spiritual lives of emerging adults.* New York, N.Y.: Oxford University Press.

Smith, C., & Denton, M. L. (2005). *Soul searching: The religious and spiritual lives of American teenagers* New York, NY: Oxford University Press.

Smith, D. I., & Smith, J. K. A. (Eds.). (2011). *Teaching and Christian practices.* Grand Rapids, MI: Wm. B. Eerdmans.

Smith, J. K. A. (2009). *Desiring the kingdom: Worship, worldview, and cultural formation (Cultural Liturgies).* Grand Rapids, MI: Baker Academic.

Smith, N. L. (2013). (Re)Considering a critical ethnorelative worldview goal and pedagogy for global and biblical demands in Christian higher education. *Christian Scholar's Review, 42*(4), 345-373.

Smithwick, D. J. (2004). *The PEERS booklet analysis package.* Lexington, KY: Nehemiah Institute, Inc.

Spurgeon, C. H. (2013). *The autobiography of Charles H. Spurgeon: Compiled from his letters, diaries, and records, 1900.* (Vol. 4). London: Forgotten (Original work published 1900).

Stake, R. E. (2010). *Qualitative research: How things work.* New York, NY: The Guilford Press.

Strauss, A., & Corbin, J. (1994). Grounded theory methodology: An overview. In N. Denzin & Y. Lincoln (Eds.), *Handbook of qualitative research* (pp. 273-285). Thousand Oaks, CA: SAGE.

———. (1998). *Basics of qualitative research: Techniques and procedures for developing grounded theory* (2nd ed.). Thousand Oaks, CA: SAGE.

Summit Pacific College - About. (2015). Retrieved from https://www.summitpacific.ca/about/

Taylor, B. B. (2009). *An altar in the world: A geography of faith.* Toronto, ON: HarperCollins.

Ter Avest, I., Bertram-Troost, G., & Miedema, S. (2012). Provocative pedagogy; Or youngsters need the brain to challenge worldview formation. *Religious Education, 107*(4), 356-370.

Thomas, D. (2014). *An exploration of the factors that influence theological students in the area of moral development and decision-making in the charismatic tradition.* (Master's thesis), University of South Africa. Retrieved from http://uir.unisa.ac.za/handle/10500/18838 Unisa Institutional Repository database.

Thomas, D. R. (2006). A general inductive approach for analyzing qualitative evaluation data. *American Journal of Evaluation, 27*(2), 237-246.

Tudge, J. (2000). Theory, method, and analysis in research on the relations between peer collaboration and cognitive development. *Journal of Experimental Education, 69,* 98-112. doi:10.1080/00220970009600651

BIBLIOGRAPHY

Urquhart, C. (2007). The evolving nature of grounded theory method: The case of the information systems discipline. In A. Bryant & K. Charmaz (Eds.), *The SAGE handbook of grounded theory*. Thousand Oaks, CA: SAGE Publications.

vanSpronsen, R. J. (2011). *Resistance, communication, and community: How did former students from an independent Christian high school experience and understand their resistance to schooling?* (Doctoral dissertation). Retrieved from http://mspace.lib.umanitoba.ca/bitstream/1993/4737/1/vanSpronsen_Rob.pdf

Walker, K. (2004). Teachers and teacher world-views. *International Education Journal, 5*(3), 433-438.

Walsh, B. J., & Middleton, J. R. (1984). *The transforming vision: Shaping a Christian worldview*. Downers Grove, Ill: InterVarsity.

Ward, T. (2012). Curriculum: The path to high-worth outcomes. *Common Ground Journal, 10*(1), 42-44.

Wilkens, S., & Sanford, M. (2009). *Hidden worldviews: Eight cultural stories that shape our lives*. Downers Grove, IL: IVP Academic.

Wilkie, S. E. (2015). *Living for eternity: A predictive analysis of manifestations of biblical worldview of university freshmen*. (Doctoral dissertation), Liberty University. Retrieved from http://digitalcommons.liberty.edu/doctoral/996

Williams, C. (2002). *Life of the mind: A Christian perspective*. Grand Rapids, MI: Baker Academic.

Wilson, E. O. (2000). *Sociobiology: The new synthesis* (25th Anniversary ed.). Cambridge, MA: The Belknap Press of Harvard University Press.

———. (1998). *Consilience: The unity of knowledge* (Reprint ed.). New York, NY: Vintage.

Wolf, S. M. (2011). The shaping of a professional worldview in the classroom: A Christian psychology project. *Journal of Psychology and Christianity, 30*(4), 329-338.

Wolterstorff, N. (1999). *Reason within the bounds of religion*. Grand Rapids, MI: Eerdman's.

———. (2002). *Educating for life: Reflections on Christian teaching and learning* (1st ed.). Grand Rapids, MI: Baker.

Wood, M. K. (2008). *A study of the worldview of K-12 Christian school educators*. (Doctoral dissertation), Liberty University, Lynchburg, VA. Retrieved from http://digitalcommons.liberty.edu/doctoral/113/

Made in the USA
Columbia, SC
16 March 2018